FLASH
in the PAN

FLASH
in the PAN

Spice Up Your Noodles & Stir-Fries

STERLING EPICURE
New York

STERLING EPICURE
New York

An Imprint of Sterling Publishing
387 Park Avenue South
New York, NY 10016

STERLING EPICURE is a trademark of Sterling Publishing Co., Inc.
The distinctive Sterling logo is a registered trademark of Sterling Publishing Co., Inc.

First published in the United Kingdom in 2013 by Pavilion Books Company Limited

ISBN 978-1-4549-1523-2

For information about custom editions, special sales, and premium and corporate purchases, please contact Sterling Special Sales at 800-805-5489 or specialsales@sterlingpublishing.com.

Manufactured in China

10 9 8 7 6 5 4 3 2 1

www.sterlingpublishing.com

NOTES

Ovens and broilers must be preheated to the specified temperature.

Large eggs should be used except where otherwise specified. Free-range eggs are recommended.

Note that some recipes contain raw or lightly cooked eggs. The young, elderly, pregnant women and anyone with an immune-deficiency disease should avoid these because of the slight risk of salmonella.

Contents

Sides and Salads

Stir-Frying Vegetables

Stir-frying is perfect for nonstarchy vegetables, as the quick cooking preserves their color, freshness, and texture.

Perfect stir-frying

- Cut everything into small pieces of uniform size so that they cook quickly and evenly.
- If you're cooking onions or garlic with the vegetables, don't keep them over high heat for too long or they will burn.
- Add all liquids toward the end of cooking so they don't evaporate.

You will need 1lb. (450g) mixed vegetables, 1–2 tbsp. vegetable oil, 2 crushed garlic cloves, 2 tbsp. soy sauce, 2 tsp. sesame oil.

1. Cut the vegetables into even-size pieces. Heat the oil in a large wok or skillet until smoking-hot. Add the garlic and cook for a few seconds, then remove and set aside.

2. Add the vegetables to the wok, then toss and stir them. Keep them moving constantly as they cook, which will take 4–5 minutes.

3. When the vegetables are just tender, but still with a slight bite, turn off the heat. Put the garlic back into the wok and stir well. Add the soy sauce and sesame oil, toss, and serve.

Stir-Fried Beans with Cherry Tomatoes

Prep time: 10 minutes
Cooking time: about 8 minutes

12oz. (350g) green beans, trimmed

2 tsp. olive oil

1 large garlic clove, crushed

5oz. (150g) cherry or grape tomatoes, halved

salt and freshly ground black pepper

2 tbsp. chopped flat leaf parsley

1 Cook the green beans in boiling salted water for 4–5 minutes, then drain well.

2 Heat the oil in a wok or large skillet over high heat. Stir-fry the beans with the garlic and tomatoes for 2–3 minutes until the beans are tender and the tomatoes are just beginning to soften without losing their shape. Season well with salt and ground black pepper, stir in the parsley, and serve.

Serves 6

Mushrooms with Cashews

Prep time: 5 minutes
Cooking time: about 8 minutes

1 tbsp. vegetable oil

2 tbsp. unsalted cashews

3¼ cups sliced cremini mushrooms

1 tbsp. lemon juice

4 tbsp. chopped fresh cilantro, plus sprigs to garnish

1 tbsp. heavy cream (optional)

1 Heat the oil in a wok or large skillet. Add the cashews and cook over high heat for 2-3 minutes until golden. Add the mushrooms and cook for 2-3 minutes longer until tender, stirring frequently.

2 Stir in the lemon juice and cilantro and season to taste with salt and ground black pepper. Cook until boiling. Remove the wok from the heat and stir in the cream if you like. Adjust the seasoning if necessary, and serve immediately, garnished with cilantro sprigs.

TRY THIS

For a simple alternative dish try **Chinese Garlic Mushrooms:** replace the nuts with 2 crushed garlic cloves and stir-fry for only 20 seconds before adding the mushrooms. Replace the lemon juice with rice wine or dry sherry.

Serves 4

Veggie Spring Rolls

Prep time: about 20 minutes
Cooking time: about 30 minutes

5oz. (150g) rice vermicelli, cooked
heaped 1 cup canned bamboo shoots
1 carrot, coarsely grated
3 scallions, thinly sliced
1 garlic clove, crushed
2 tbsp. soy sauce
salt and freshly ground black pepper
1 tbsp. oil, plus extra to brush
large handful fresh cilantro,
    finely chopped
1–2 tsp. toasted sesame oil
6 x 8in. (20cm) square spring roll
    wrappers, thawed if frozen

1 Heat oven to 400°F (350°F for convection ovens). Roughly chop the vermicelli into bite-size pieces, then put into a large bowl. Roughly cut the bamboo shoots into matchsticks and add to the vermicelli with the carrot, scallions, garlic, soy sauce, and some salt and pepper.

2 Heat the oil in a large wok or skillet over high heat. Add the vermicelli mixture and cook for a few minutes, stirring occasionally, until the vegetables are tender. Remove from the heat and leave to cool.

3 Mix in the cilantro and sesame oil; check the seasoning. Put a spring roll wrapper on a cutting board and spoon one-sixth of the vermicelli mixture along one edge, leaving a 1in. (2.5cm) border on each side. Fold in the sides over the filling, then roll up (encasing the filling), sealing with a little water. Repeat with remaining mixture and wrappers.

4 Arrange the spring rolls seam-side down on a nonstick baking sheet and brush with oil. Cook in the oven for 20–25 minutes until golden brown. Let cool for a few minutes, then serve with sweet chili sauce.

The Asian Pantry

Rice and noodles are the staple foods across Asia. The following ingredients, used in many Asian dishes, are available in most large supermarkets and Asian food stores.

Spices

- **Chinese five-spice powder** is made from star anise, fennel seeds, cinnamon, cloves, and Sichuan pepper. It has a strong licoricelike flavor and should be used sparingly.
- **Kaffir lime leaves**, used in Southeast Asian cooking for their lime-lemon flavor, are glossy leaves used whole but not eaten—rather like bay leaves. Use grated lime zest as a substitute.
- **Tamarind paste** has a delicately sour flavor; use lemon juice as a substitute.

Sauces

- **Soy sauce**—made from fermented soybeans and, usually, wheat—is the most common flavoring in Chinese and Southeast Asian cooking. There are light and dark soy sauces; the dark kind is slightly sweeter and tends to darken the food. Both will keep indefinitely.
- **Thai fish sauce** is a salty condiment with a distinctive, pungent aroma. It is used in many Southeast Asian dishes. You can buy it in most large supermarkets and Asian food stores. It will keep indefinitely.
- **Thai green curry paste** is a blend of spices, such as green chilies, cilantro, and lemongrass. Thai red curry paste contains fresh and dried red chilies and ginger. Once opened, store in a sealed container in the refrigerator for up to one month.
- **Chili sauce** is made from fresh red chilies, vinegar, salt, and sugar; some versions include other ingredients, such as garlic or ginger. Sweet chili sauce is a useful standby for adding piquancy to all kinds of dishes.
- **Black bean sauce** is made from fermented black beans, salt, and ginger. Salty and pungent on its own, it adds richness to many stir-fry dishes.
- **Yellow bean sauce** is a thick, salty, aromatic yellow-brown puree of fermented yellow soybeans, flour, and salt.
- **Hoisin sauce**, sometimes called barbecue sauce, is a thick, sweet-spicy red-brown sauce made from mashed soybeans, garlic, chilies, and other spices.
- **Oyster sauce** is a smooth brown sauce made from oyster extract, wheat flour, and other flavorings. It doesn't taste fishy, but adds a "meaty" flavor to stir-fries and braised dishes.
- **Plum sauce**, made from plums, ginger, chilies, vinegar, and sugar, is traditionally served with duck or as a dip.

Coconut milk

- **Canned coconut milk** is widely available. It adds a rich creaminess to braised dishes. You can also use blocks of creamed coconut or coconut powder, following the package directions, to make the amount of liquid you need.

Canned vegetables

- **Bamboo shoots**, available sliced or in chunks, have a mild flavor; rinse before use.
- **Water chestnuts** have a very mild flavor, but add a crunch to stir-fried and braised dishes.

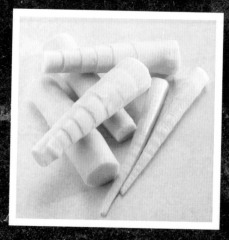

Other ingredients

- **Dried mushrooms** feature in some Chinese recipes; they need to be soaked in hot water for 30 minutes before use.
- **Dried shrimp and dried shrimp paste (blachan)** are often used in Southeast Asian cooking. The pungent smell becomes milder during cooking and marries with the other ingredients. These are often included in bottled sauces and spice pastes, and are not suitable for vegetarians.
- **Mirin** is a sweet rice wine from Japan; if you can't find it, use dry or medium sherry instead.
- **Rice wine** is often used in Chinese cooking; if you can't find it, use dry sherry instead.
- **Rice vinegar** is clear and milder than other vinegars. Use white wine vinegar or apple cider vinegar as a substitute.

Which oil to use?

- **Peanut** oil has a mild flavor and is widely used in China and Southeast Asia. It is well suited to stir-frying and deep-frying, because it has a high smoke point and can, therefore, be used at high temperatures.
- **Vegetable oil** can be pure canola oil, or a blend of corn, soybean, canola, or other oils. It usually has a bland flavor and is suitable for stir-frying.
- **Sesame oil** has a distinctive nutty flavor; it is best used in marinades or added as a seasoning to stir-fried dishes just before serving.

Sesame and Cabbage Rolls

Prep time: 30 minutes, plus soaking
Cooking time: about 15 minutes, plus cooling

2oz. (50g) dried shiitake mushrooms
3 tbsp. sesame oil
4 garlic cloves, crushed
4 tbsp. sesame seeds
6½ cups finely shredded cabbage
1 bunch of scallions, trimmed
  and chopped
2 cups canned bamboo shoots, drained
3 tbsp. soy sauce
½ tsp. sugar
1lb. 2oz. (500g) phyllo pastry dough,
  thawed if frozen
1 extra-large egg, beaten
vegetable oil for deep-frying
spiced plum sauce or Thai chili sauce
  to serve

1 Put the mushrooms in a heatproof
  bowl, cover with boiling water, and
  let soak for 20 minutes.
2 Heat the sesame oil in a wok or
  large skillet. Add the garlic and
  sesame seeds and fry slowly until
  golden brown. Add the cabbage and
  scallions and stir-fry for 3 minutes.

3 Drain and slice the mushrooms. Add
  them to the wok with the bamboo
  shoots, soy sauce, and sugar and stir
  until well mixed. Remove the pan
  from the heat and let cool.
4 Cut the phyllo pastry dough into
  twenty-four 7in. (18cm) squares.
  Keep the phyllo squares covered
  with a damp dish towel as you work.
  Place one phyllo square on the work
  surface and cover with a second
  square. Place a heaping tablespoon
  of the cabbage mixture across the
  middle of the top square to within
  1in. (2.5cm) of the ends. Fold the
  1in. (2.5cm) ends of phyllo over the
  filling. Brush one unfolded edge
  of the phyllo with a little egg, then
  roll up to make a thick roll. Shape
  the remaining phyllo and filling the
  same way to make 12 rolls.
5 Heat 2in. (5cm) oil in a deep-fryer
  or large heavy-bottomed saucepan
  to 350°F. (Test by frying a small
  cube of bread; it should brown in

Makes 12

40 seconds.) Fry the rolls in batches for about 3 minutes until crisp and golden. Remove with a slotted spoon and drain on paper towels; keep them warm while you fry the remaining rolls. Serve hot with a sauce for dipping.

Perfect Deep-Frying

Shellfish and small pieces of fish, carrots, broccoli, onions, zucchini, eggplant, mushrooms, bell peppers, and cauliflower are all good deep-fried in a light batter.

To serve four, you will need: About 2lb. (900g) mixed vegetables, such as broccoli, cauliflower, eggplant, and red peppers, cut into small, similar-size pieces; vegetable oil to deep-fry; 1 cup all-purpose flour, plus extra to coat; 1 cup cornstarch; a pinch of salt; 1 egg yolk, 1¼ cups (300ml) sparkling water.

1 Prepare the vegetables and cut into small pieces, no larger than ¾in. (2cm) thick. Dry well on paper towels.
2 Heat the oil in a deep-fryer to 375°F. (A small cube of bread should brown in 40 seconds.)

3 To make the batter, lightly whisk together the flour, cornstarch, salt, egg yolk, and water.

4 Coat the vegetables lightly with flour, then dip into the batter.

5 Fry in batches, a few pieces at a time, until the batter is crisp and golden brown. Don't put too many vegetables in the pan at once (if you do, the temperature drops and the vegetables take longer to cook and become greasy). Remove with a slotted spoon and drain on paper towels before serving.

Vegetable Tempura

Prep time: 20 minutes
Cooking time: 15 minutes

1 cup all-purpose flour, plus 2 tbsp.
   extra to sprinkle
2 tbsp. cornstarch
2 tbsp. arrowroot starch
salt and freshly ground black pepper
1¼ cups small cauliflower, florets
2 large carrots, cut into matchsticks
16 button mushrooms
2 zucchini, sliced
2 red bell peppers, seeded and sliced
vegetable oil to deep-fry
fresh cilantro sprigs to garnish

For the dipping sauce:

2 tbsp. grated fresh ginger
4 tbsp. dry sherry
3 tbsp. soy sauce

1 Sift the flour, cornstarch, and
arrowroot starch into a large bowl
with a pinch each of salt and ground
black pepper. Gradually whisk
in 1¼ cups (300ml) ice-cold water
to form a thin batter. Cover the bowl
and chill in the refrigerator.

2 To make the dipping sauce, put
the ginger, sherry, and soy sauce
in a heatproof bowl and add ¾ cup
plus 2 tbsp. boiling water. Stir well
to mix, then set aside.

3 Put the vegetables in a large bowl
and sprinkle with 2 tbsp. flour. Toss
well to coat. Heat the oil in a wok
or deep-fryer to 375°F. (Test by
frying a small cube of bread;
it should brown in 40 seconds.)

4 Dip a handful of the vegetables into
the batter, then remove with
a slotted spoon, taking up a lot
of the batter with the vegetables.
Add to the hot oil and deep-fry for
3–5 minutes until crisp and golden.
Remove with a slotted spoon and
drain on paper towels; keep them
hot while you cook the remaining
batches. Serve immediately,
garnished with cilantro sprigs and
accompanied by the dipping sauce.

Serves 4

Thai Noodle Salad

Prep time: 20 minutes, plus soaking
Cooking time: about 8 minutes

2 cups sugar snap peas, trimmed

9oz. (250g) Thai stir-fry rice noodles

¾ cup cashews

2 cups carrots cut into matchsticks

10 scallions, sliced on the diagonal

3 cups bean sprouts

2 tbsp. roughly chopped fresh cilantro,
plus sprigs to garnish

1 red bird's-eye chili, seeded and finely
chopped (see Safety Tip, page 28)

2 tsp. sweet chili sauce

4 tbsp. sesame oil

6 tbsp. soy sauce

juice of 2 limes

salt and freshly ground black pepper

1 Bring a pot of salted water to a boil and blanch the sugar snap peas for 2–3 minutes until just tender. Drain and refresh under cold water.

2 Put the noodles into a bowl, cover with boiling water and let soak for 4 minutes, or according to the package directions. Rinse under cold water and drain very well.

3 Toast the cashews in a dry skillet until golden—about 5 minutes.

4 Put the sugar snaps in a large glass serving bowl. Add the carrots, scallions, bean sprouts, cilantro, chili, cashews, and noodles. Mix together the chili sauce, oil, soy sauce, and lime juice, and season well with salt and ground black pepper. Pour over the salad, toss together, garnish with cilantro sprigs, and serve.

COOK'S TIP

Red bird's-eye chilies are always very hot. The smaller they are, the hotter they are.

Serves 4

Shrimp and Noodle Salad

Prep time: 15 minutes

11oz. (300g) ready-to-stir-fry rice
  noodles

juice of 2 limes

1 tbsp. Thai fish sauce

2 tsp. light brown sugar

1 red chili, seeded and finely chopped
  (see Safety Tip)

1in. (2.5cm) piece of fresh ginger,
  peeled and grated

2 carrots, peeled into ribbons

3 cups bean sprouts

2 cups sugar snap peas sliced
  lengthwise

12oz. (350g) cooked shrimp, shelled
  and deveined

handful of fresh mint leaves, chopped

3 tbsp. roughly chopped roasted
  salted peanuts

1 Put the rice noodles into a heatproof
  bowl and pour boiling water over
  them until they are covered. Cover
  with plastic wrap. Set aside for
  5 minutes to heat through. Drain
  well and put back into the bowl.

2 In a separate bowl, stir together the
  lime juice, fish sauce, sugar, chili,
  and ginger. Add the vegetables,
  shrimp, and mint to the drained
  noodles, then pour the dressing
  over and toss well. Garnish with
  peanuts and serve.

SAFETY TIP

Chilies can be very mild to
blisteringly hot, depending on the
type of chili and its ripeness. Taste
a small piece first to check it's not
too hot for you. Be extremely careful
when handling chilies not to touch
or rub your eyes with your fingers,
or they will sting. Wash knives
immediately after chopping chilies.
As a precaution, use rubber gloves
when preparing them, if you like.

Serves 4

Chili and Beef Noodle Salad

Prep time: 15 minutes, plus soaking

5oz. (150g) dried rice noodles

large handful of arugula

4oz. (125g) cold roast beef, cut into
   thin strips

1½ cups chopped roasted
   or sun-dried tomatoes

For the Thai dressing:

juice of 1 lime

1 lemongrass stalk, outside leaves
   discarded, finely chopped

1 red chili, seeded and chopped (see
   Safety Tip, page 28)

2 tsp. finely chopped fresh ginger

2 garlic cloves, crushed

1 tbsp. Thai fish sauce

3 tbsp. extra virgin olive oil

salt and freshly ground black pepper

TRY THIS

For an easy alternative, use roast
pork instead of beef.

1 Put the noodles in a large bowl and
pour boiling water over them
to cover and leave to soak.

2 To make the dressing, whisk
together the lime juice, lemongrass,
chili, ginger, garlic, fish sauce, and
oil in a small bowl and season with
salt and ground black pepper.

3 While the noodles are still warm,
drain them well, then put in a large
bowl and toss with the dressing.
Let cool.

4 Just before serving, add the arugula,
sliced beef, and tomatoes to the
noodles and toss well.

Serves 4

Soups and Curries

Chicken Noodle Soup

Prep time: 15 minutes
Cooking time: 23 minutes

2 eggs

1⅔ quarts (1.6 liters) chicken stock

1 tbsp. light soy sauce

¾ in. (2cm) piece of fresh ginger,
   thickly sliced

1 garlic clove, crushed

3 boneless, skinless chicken
   breast halves

2 carrots, finely chopped

4oz. (125g) fine or medium egg
   noodles

salt and freshly ground black pepper

2 cups oyster mushrooms

4 scallions, finely sliced, to garnish

1 Bring a small pot of water to a boil;
  then simmer the eggs for 7 minutes.
  Drain, put in a bowl, and cover with
  cold water.

2 Meanwhile, heat the chicken stock,
  soy sauce, ginger, and garlic
  in a large pot and bring to a boil.
  Add the chicken, reduce the heat
  and simmer for 12 minutes, or until
  the meat is cooked through. Lift the
  meat out of the broth and onto
  a cutting board. Discard the ginger
  and garlic. Add the carrots and
  noodles to the broth. Simmer for
  4 minutes and season to taste with
  salt and pepper. Meanwhile, slice
  the chicken breast and shell and
  halve the eggs.

3 Divide the soup among four warm
  bowls, adding a little more hot stock
  if needed. Top each with one-quarter
  of the chicken slices, one-quarter
  of the mushrooms, and half an egg.
  Garnish with the sliced scallions
  and serve.

TRY THIS

This Japanese-style soup is full
of light flavors—add a chopped
red chili, if you like, for an easy
way to spice it up.

Serves 4

Spicy Beef and Noodle Soup

Prep time: 10 minutes, plus soaking
Cooking time: 10 minutes

½ oz. (15g) dried porcini or
   shiitake mushrooms
2 tbsp. peanut oil
8oz. (225g) boneless flank steak, cut
   into thin strips
4½ cups (1.1 liters) beef stock
2 tbsp. Thai fish sauce (nam pla), plus
   extra if needed
1 large fresh red chili, seeded and
   finely chopped (see Safety Tip,
   page 28)
1 lemongrass stalk, outer leaves
   discard, thinly sliced
1in. (2.5cm) piece of fresh ginger,
   peeled and finely chopped
6 scallions, halved lengthwise and cut
   into 1in. (2.5cm) pieces
1 garlic clove, crushed
¼ tsp. sugar
2oz. (50g) medium egg noodles
2¼ cups roughly fresh spinach leaves
4 tbsp. chopped fresh cilantro
freshly ground black pepper

1 Break the dried mushrooms into
pieces, then soak in ⅔ cup (150ml)
boiling water for 15 minutes.

2 Meanwhile, heat the oil in a large
pot over medium heat. Brown the
meat in two batches and set aside.
Pour the stock into the pot with
2 tbsp. fish sauce. Add the
mushrooms and their soaking
liquid, the chili, lemongrass, ginger,
scallions, garlic, and sugar. Bring
to a boil.

3 Break the noodles up slightly and
add to the pot, then stir gently until
they begin to separate. Reduce the
heat and simmer for 4–5 minutes
until the noodles are just tender,
stirring occasionally.

4 Stir in the spinach, cilantro, and
reserved steak. Check and adjust
the seasoning with ground black
pepper, and add a little more fish
sauce if necessary. Spoon into four
warm bowls and serve hot.

Serves 4

Perfect Wok

You don't need to buy special equipment to start stir-frying—a large, deep-sided skillet and a spatula will do the job—but a wok is very versatile, with many uses in the kitchen.

Choosing a wok

Traditional steel woks have rounded bottoms, so the food always returns to the middle where the heat is most intense. The deep side prevent the food from falling out during stir-frying. Most woks now have flattened bottoms, which makes them more stable on modern stovetops. Nonstick woks are widely available; they are easy to clean and not prone to rusting.

- There are two main styles of wok, one with double handles opposite each other, the other with one long handle. The double-handled wok gets very hot and needs to be handled with oven mitts, although it is slightly more stable if you use it for steaming and braising.

- A wok with a long single handle is the best choice as it is easier to manipulate when stir-frying.
- A wok with a diameter of 14in. (35.5cm) is most useful for cooking stir-fries for four people.
- A tight-fitting lid is useful if you intend to use your wok for steaming as well as stir-frying.

Wok equipment

Wok spoon A metal utensil with a curved end to match the curve of the wok is useful for stir-frying in a traditional steel wok, but should not be used in nonstick woks—any heatproof spatula will do.

Chopsticks Long wooden chopsticks are great for stir-frying in nonstick woks; they are also useful for separating blocks of noodles as they cook.

Steamers come in various sizes, and can be of bamboo or pierced metal. They can be used in a wok or over a pan of boiling water, covered with a tight-fitting lid.

Trivet or steamer rack A wooden or metal trivet or steamer rack fits inside the wok to keep food above the water level when steaming.

Wok stand A wok stand or ring, which sits on the stovetop with the wok on top, helps keep the wok stable during steaming or braising.

Strainer A long-handled strainer is useful for scooping food from deep-frying oil, but a slotted spoon can be used instead.

Seasoning a wok

Nonstick woks do not need to be seasoned. Traditional steel woks, designed to withstand high temperatures, can be made practically nonstick by "seasoning" before you use them for the first time. First scrub the wok in hot water and detergent, then dry thoroughly with paper towels. Place it over low heat, add 2 tbsp. peanut oil, and rub this over the entire inner surface with paper towels. Keep the wok over low heat until the oil starts to smoke. Let cool for 5 minutes, then rub well with paper towels. Add another 2 tbsp. oil and repeat the heating process twice more until the paper towel wipes clean. The wok is now seasoned. If used regularly it should remain rust-free. After each use, rinse in hot water—but not detergent—and wipe clean with paper towels. If you scrub your wok or use detergent you will need to season it again.

Chicken and Coconut Curry

Prep time: 15 minutes
Cooking time: 35 minutes

2 garlic cloves, peeled

1 onion, quartered

1 lemongrass stalk, halved

1in. (2.5cm) piece of fresh ginger, peeled and halved

2 small hot chilies (see Safety Tip, page 28)

a small handful of fresh cilantro

1 tsp. ground coriander

grated zest and juice of 1 lime

2 tbsp. vegetable oil

6 boneless, skinless chicken breast halves, each cut into three pieces

2 large tomatoes, peeled and chopped

2 tbsp. Thai fish sauce

3¾ cups (900ml) coconut milk

salt and freshly ground black pepper

finely sliced red chili to garnish (see Safety Tip, page 28)

basmati rice to serve

1 Put the garlic, onion, lemongrass, ginger, chilies, cilantro, ground coriander, and lime zest and juice in a food processor and blend to a paste. Add a little water if the mixture gets stuck under the blades.

2 Heat the oil in a wok or large skillet. Add the spice paste and cook over medium-high heat for 3–4 minutes, stirring constantly. Add the chicken and cook for 5 minutes, stirring to coat in the spice mixture.

3 Add the tomatoes, fish sauce, and coconut milk. Simmer, covered, for about 25 minutes, or until the chicken is cooked through. Season with salt and ground black pepper, garnish with red chili and serve with basmati rice.

Serves 6

Thai Red Seafood Curry

Prep time: 15 minutes
Cooking time: about 10 minutes

1 tbsp. vegetable oil
3 tbsp. Thai red curry paste
1lb. (450g) monkfish tail, boned
  to make a 12oz. (350g) fillet, sliced
  crosswise
12oz. (350g) raw large, shelled
  shrimp, deveined
1 can (15-oz./425g) low-fat coconut
  milk
¾ cup plus 2 tbsp fish stock
juice of 1 lime
1–2 tbsp. Thai fish sauce
1¼ cups snow peas
3 tbsp. fresh cilantro, roughly torn
salt and freshly ground black pepper

1 Heat the oil in a wok or large
nonstick skillet. Add the curry paste
and cook for 1–2 minutes.

2 Add the monkfish and shrimp and
stir well to coat in the curry paste.
Add the coconut milk, stock, lime
juice, and fish sauce. Stir all the
ingredients together and bring
just to a boil.

3 Add the snow peas, reduce the heat,
and simmer for 5 minutes, or until
the snow peas and fish are tender.
Stir in the cilantro and check
the seasoning, adding salt and
ground black pepper to taste.
Serve immediately.

SAVE MONEY

If you can't find low-fat coconut
milk, use half a can of full-fat
coconut milk and make up the
difference with water or stock.
Freeze the remaining milk for up
to one month.

Fish Curry

Prep time: 20 minutes
Cooking time: about 25 minutes

1 tsp. vegetable oil

2 onions, thinly sliced

2in. (5cm) piece of fresh ginger, peeled and grated

1 tsp. each ground turmeric and coriander

1 tbsp. medium curry paste

4 tomatoes, roughly chopped

1¾ cups (400ml) fish stock

7oz. (200g) raw shelled shrimp

11oz. (300g) white skinless fish, such as cod, haddock, or pollock, cut into 1in. (2.5cm) cubes

1½ cups frozen peas

salt and freshly ground black pepper

boiled rice or crusty bread to serve

1 Heat the oil in a large pan over low heat. Add the onions and a good pinch of salt, then cover and cook for 15 minutes, or until completely softened. Stir in the ginger, turmeric, coriander, and curry paste. Cook for 1 minute.

2 Stir in the tomatoes and stock and simmer for 5 minutes. Mix in the shrimp, fish, and peas, then cook for 3–5 minutes, stirring carefully to prevent the fish from breaking up, until the shrimp are bright pink, and the fish is opaque. Season to taste with salt and black pepper and serve with rice or crusty bread, if you like.

HEALTHY TIP

If you're trying to up your vegetable intake, fold through a few large handfuls of spinach just before serving.

Serves 4

Thai Green Shellfish Curry

Prep time: 10 minutes
Cooking time: about 15 minutes

1 tbsp. vegetable oil
1 lemongrass stalk, chopped
2 small red chilies, chopped (see
   Safety Tip, page 28)
a handful of fresh cilantro leaves,
   chopped, plus extra to serve
2 kaffir lime leaves, chopped
1–2 tbsp. Thai green curry paste
1 can (15-oz./425ml) coconut milk
2 cups vegetable stock
salt and freshly ground black pepper
14oz. (400g) medium scallops,
   preferably with roe attached
9oz. (250g) raw jumbo shelled shrimp,
   deveined, with tails intact
jasmine rice to serve

1 Heat the oil in a wok or large skillet. Add the lemongrass, chilies, cilantro, and lime leaves and stir-fry for 30 seconds. Add the curry paste and stir-fry for 1 minute longer.

2 Add the coconut milk and stock and bring to a boil. Reduce the heat and simmer for 5–10 minutes until slightly reduced. Season well with salt and ground black pepper.

3 Add the scallops and shrimp and bring just to a boil, then reduce the heat and simmer gently for 2–3 minutes until cooked. Divide the jasmine rice among six serving bowls and spoon the curry over the top. Sprinkle with cilantro and serve immediately.

TRY THIS

For an easy alternative, use
cleaned squid or mussels
instead of scallops and shrimp.

Thai Green Curry

Prep time: 10 minutes
Cooking time: 15 minutes

2 tsp. vegetable oil

1 green chili, seeded and finely
chopped (see Safety Tip, page 28)

1½in. (4cm) piece of fresh ginger,
peeled and finely grated

1 lemongrass stalk, cut into
three pieces

8oz. (225g) cremini or oyster
mushrooms

1 tbsp. Thai green curry paste

1¼ cups (300ml) coconut milk

⅔ cup (150ml) chicken stock

1 tbsp. Thai fish sauce

1 tsp. light soy sauce

12oz. (350g) boneless, skinless chicken
breast halves, cut into
bite-size pieces

12oz. (350g) cooked large, shelled
shrimp

fresh cilantro sprigs to garnish

1 Heat the oil in a wok or large skillet. Add the chili, ginger, lemongrass, and mushrooms and stir-fry for about 3 minutes, or until the mushrooms begin to turn golden. Add the curry paste and fry for 1 minute longer.

2 Pour in the coconut milk, stock, fish sauce, and soy sauce and bring to a boil. Stir in the chicken, reduce the heat, and simmer for about 8 minutes until the chicken is cooked through. Add the shrimp and cook for 1 minute longer, stirring. Garnish with cilantro sprigs and serve immediately.

Serves 6

Ginger

Grating

1 Cut off a piece of the root and peel with a vegetable peeler. Cut off any brown spots.
2 Rest the grater on a board or small plate and grate the ginger. Discard any large fibers sticking to the pulp.

Slicing, shredding, and chopping

Cut slices off the ginger and cut off the skin carefully. Cut off any brown spots. Stack the slices and cut into shreds. To chop, stack the shreds of ginger and cut across into small pieces.

Pressing

If you just need the ginger juice, peel and cut off any brown spots, then cut into small chunks and use a garlic press held over a small bowl to extract the juice.

Garlic

Removing the Skin

1 Put the clove on a cutting board and place the flat side of a large knife on top of it. Press down firmly on the flat of the blade to crush the clove and break the papery skin.
2 Cut off the bottom of the clove and slip the garlic out of its skin. It should come away easily.

Crushing

After step 2 above, the whole clove can be put into a garlic press. To crush with a knife: roughly chop the peeled cloves with a pinch of salt. Press down hard with the edge of a large knife tip, with the blade facing away from you, then drag the blade along the garlic while still pressing hard. Continue to do this, dragging the knife tip over the garlic.

Slicing

Using a rocking motion with the knife tip on the board, slice the garlic as thinly as you need.

Shredding and chopping

Holding the slices together, shred them across the slices. Chop the shreds if you need chopped garlic.

Chilies

1 Cut off the stem and slit open lengthwise. Using a spoon, scrape out the seeds and pith.
2 For diced chili, cut into thin shreds lengthwise, then cut crosswise.

Cook's Tip: Wash your hands thoroughly after handling chilies —the volatile oils will sting if they are accidentally rubbed into your eyes.

Cilantro

Cilantro, also known as Chinese parsley, is the most commonly used herb throughout Asia. In Thailand the roots are often used in curry pastes.

1 Trim off any roots and the lower part of the stems. Immerse in cold water and shake briskly. Leave in the water for a few minutes.
2 Lift out of the water and put in a colander or sieve, then rinse again under cold running water. Let drain for a few minutes, then dry thoroughly on paper or dish towels, or use a salad spinner.

Note: Don't pour the herbs and their water into the sieve, because dirt in the water might get caught in the leaves.
3 Gather the leaves into a compact ball in one hand, keeping your fist around the ball, but being careful not to crush them. Chop with a large knife, using a rocking motion and letting just a little of the ball out of your fingers at a time.
4 When the herbs are roughly chopped, continue chopping until the pieces are as fine as you need.

Lemongrass

Lemongrass is a popular Southeast Asian ingredient, giving an aromatic lemony flavor. It looks rather like a long, slender scallion, but is fibrous and woody, and is usually removed before the dish is served. Alternatively, the inner leaves can be very finely chopped or pounded in a mortar and pestle and used in spice pastes.

Thai Red Turkey Curry

Prep time: 20 minutes
Cooking time: about 25 minutes

3 tbsp. vegetable oil

3 cups finely chopped onions

7oz. (200g) green beans, trimmed

4oz. (125g) baby sweet corn cobs, cut on the diagonal

2 red bell peppers, seeded and cut into thick slices

1 tbsp. Thai red curry paste, or to taste

1 red chili, seeded and finely chopped (see Safety Tip, page 28)

1 lemongrass stalk, very finely chopped

4 kaffir lime leaves, bruised

2 tbsp. peeled and finely chopped fresh ginger

1 garlic clove, crushed

1¾ cups coconut milk

2½ cups chicken or turkey stock

3¼ cups cooked turkey cut into strips

1½ cups bean sprouts

fresh basil leaves to garnish

1 Heat the oil in a wok or large skillet. Add the onions and cook for 4–5 minutes until soft.

2 Add the beans, baby corn, and peppers to the pan and stir-fry for 3–4 minutes. Add the curry paste, chili, lemongrass, kaffir lime leaves, ginger, and garlic and cook for 2 minutes longer, stirring. Remove from the pan and set aside.

3 Add the coconut milk and stock to the pan, bring to a boil, and boil vigorously for 5–10 minutes until reduced by one-quarter.

4 Put the vegetables back into the pan with the turkey and bean sprouts. Bring to a boil, reduce the heat, and simmer for 1–2 minutes until heated through. Serve immediately, garnished with basil leaves.

SAVE MONEY

This is a great way to use up leftover turkey.

Serves 6

Hot Jungle Curry

Prep time: 10 minutes
Cooking time: about 20 minutes

1 tbsp. vegetable oil

2½ cups boneless, skinless chicken
breast halves, cut into strips

2 tbsp. Thai red curry paste

1in. (2.5cm) piece of fresh ginger,
peeled and thinly sliced

1½ cups eggplant cut into
bite-size pieces

4oz. (125g) baby corn cobs, halved
lengthwise

3oz. (75g) green beans, trimmed

3oz. (75g) button or cremini
mushrooms, halved if large

2–3 kaffir lime leaves (optional)

2 cups chicken stock

2 tbsp. Thai fish sauce

grated zest of ½ lime, plus extra
to garnish

1 tsp. tomato paste

1 tbsp. brown sugar

1 Heat the oil in a wok or large skillet.
Add the chicken and cook, stirring,
for 5 minutes, or until the chicken
turns golden brown.

2 Add the red curry paste and
cook for 1 minute longer. Add the
ginger, eggplant, baby corn, beans,
mushrooms, and lime leaves, if you
like, and stir until coated in the red
curry paste. Add all the remaining
ingredients and bring to a boil.
Reduce the heat and simmer gently
for 10–12 minutes until the chicken
and vegetables are just tender. Serve
immediately, sprinkled with
lime zest.

TRY THIS

Add 2 cups drained canned
bamboo shoots with the other
vegetables in step 2, if you like.

Serves 4

Lamb and Bamboo Shoot Red Curry

Prep time: 10 minutes
Cooking time: about 45 minutes

2 tbsp. sunflower oil

1 large onion, cut into wedges

2 garlic cloves, finely chopped

1lb. (450g) lean boneless lamb, cut into
  1¼in. (3cm) cubes

2 tbsp. Thai red curry paste

⅔ cup (150ml) lamb or beef stock

2 tbsp. Thai fish sauce

2 tsp. brown sugar

1½ cups drained and thinly sliced
  canned bamboo slices

1 red bell pepper, seeded and
  thinly sliced

2 tbsp. chopped fresh mint

1 tbsp. chopped fresh basil

2 tbsp. unsalted peanuts, toasted

boiled rice to serve

1 Heat the oil in a wok or large skillet. Add the onion and garlic and stir-fry over medium heat for 5 minutes.

2 Add the lamb and the curry paste and stir-fry for 5 minutes longer. Add the stock, fish sauce, and sugar. Bring to a boil, then reduce the heat, cover, and simmer for 20 minutes.

3 Stir the bamboo shoots, red pepper, and herbs into the curry and simmer, uncovered, for 10 minutes longer. Stir in the peanuts and serve immediately, with rice.

Serves 4

Thai Beef Curry

Prep time: 20 minutes
Cooking time: about 30 minutes, plus cooling

4 cloves

1 tsp. coriander seeds

1 tsp. cumin seeds

seeds from 3 cardamom pods

2 garlic cloves, roughly chopped

1in. (2.5cm) piece of fresh ginger, peeled and roughly chopped

1 small onion, roughly chopped

2 tbsp. sunflower oil

1 tbsp. sesame oil

1 tbsp. Thai red curry paste

1 tsp. ground turmeric

1lb. (450g) sirloin steak, cut into 1¼in. (3cm) cubes

8oz. (225g) waxy potatoes, quartered

4 tomatoes, quartered

1 tsp. sugar

1 tbsp. light soy sauce

1¼ cups (300ml) coconut milk

⅔ cup (150ml) beef stock

4 small red chilies, bruised (see Safety Tip, page 28)

4 tbsp. cashews

boiled rice and stir-fried green vegetables to serve

1 Put the cloves, coriander, cumin, and cardamom seeds in a small, heavy skillet and stir-fry over high heat for 1–2 minutes until fragrant. Do not let them burn. Cool slightly, then grind to a powder in a spice grinder.

2 Put the garlic, ginger, and onion in a food processor and blend to form a smooth paste. Heat the oils in a wok or deep skillet. Add the onion paste and curry paste and stir-fry for 5 minutes. Add the ground roasted spices and turmeric and stir-fry for 5 minutes longer.

3 Add the beef to the pan and fry for 5 minutes, or until browned on all sides. Add the potatoes, tomatoes, sugar, soy sauce, coconut milk, stock, and chilies to the pan. Bring to a boil, then reduce the heat, cover, and simmer for about 15 minutes until the beef is tender and the potatoes are cooked.

4 Stir in the cashews and serve the curry with rice and stir-fried green vegetables.

Serves 4

Salmon Laksa Curry

🍴 **Prep time:** 10 minutes
Cooking time: about 20 minutes

1 tbsp. olive oil
1 onion, thinly sliced
3 tbsp. laksa paste
¾ cup plus 2 tbsp. coconut milk
3¾ cups vegetable stock, hot
7oz. (200g) baby corn cobs,
　halved lengthwise
salt and freshly ground black pepper
1lb. 5oz. (600g) piece skinless salmon
　fillet, cut into ½in. (1cm) slices
4 cups baby spinach, washed
9oz. (250g) medium rice noodles
2 scallions, sliced diagonally,
　2 tbsp. chopped fresh cilantro, and
　1 lime, cut into wedges, to garnish

1 Heat the oil in a wok or large skillet.
Add the onion and fry over medium
heat for 10 minutes, stirring, until
golden. Add the laksa paste and fry,
stirring, for 2 minutes longer.

2 Add the coconut milk, stock, and
baby corn and season with salt and
pepper. Bring to a boil, reduce the
heat, and simmer for 5 minutes.

3 Add the salmon slices and spinach,
stirring to immerse them in the
liquid. Cook for 4 minutes until the
fish is opaque all the way through
and flakes easily.

4 Meanwhile, put the noodles into
a large heatproof bowl, cover
with boiling water, and soak for
30 seconds, or according to package
directions. Drain well, then stir
them into the curry.

5 Pour the curry into four warm
serving bowls and garnish with the
scallions, cilantro, and lime wedges.
Serve immediately.

TRY THIS

Laksa paste is a hot-and-spicy
Thai paste, but you can use Thai
curry paste instead.

Serves 4

Rice and Noodles

Perfect Rice

Perfectly cooked rice can be a quick accompaniment or a meal in itself. Follow these simple steps for perfect results every time.

Cooking rice

There are two main types of rice: long grain and short grain. Long-grain rice is generally served as an accompaniment; the most commonly used type of long-grain rice in Southeast Asian cooking is jasmine rice, also known as Thai fragrant rice. It has a distinctive taste and slightly sticky texture. Long-grain rice does not need any special preparation, although it should be washed to remove excess starch. Put the rice in a bowl and cover with cold water. Stir until this becomes cloudy, then drain and repeat until the water is clear.

Long-grain rice

1 Measure the rice (see right) with a cup measure and put it in a pan with a pinch of salt and twice the volume of boiling water or stock.

1

2. Bring to a boil. Reduce the heat to low and set the timer for the time stated on the package. The rice should be al dente: tender with a bite at the middle.

3. When the rice is cooked, fluff the grains with a fork.

Basmati rice

Put the rice in a bowl and cover with cold water. Stir until this becomes cloudy, then drain and repeat until the water is clear. Soak the rice for 30 minutes, then drain before cooking.

Perfect rice

- Use 2–3oz. (50–75g) raw rice per person—measured with a cup measure this is ¼–scant ½ cup.
- If you cook rice often, you might want to invest in a special rice steamer. They are available in Asian supermarkets and some kitchenware stores, and give good, consistent results.

Simple Fried Rice

TAKE 5

🍴 **Prep time:** 5 minutes
🍴 **Cooking time:** about 20 minutes

¾ cup long-grain rice

2 tbsp. sesame oil

3 eggs, lightly beaten

scant 2 cups frozen baby peas

9oz. (250g) cooked shelled shrimp

1 Cook the rice in boiling water for 10 minutes, or according to the package directions. Drain well.

2 Heat 1 tsp. oil in a large, nonstick skillet. Pour in half the beaten eggs and tilt the pan around over the heat for 1 minute, or until the egg is set. Transfer the omelet onto a warm plate. Repeat with another 1 tsp. sesame oil and the remaining beaten egg to make a second omelet. Transfer to another warm plate.

3 Add the remaining oil to the pan and stir in the rice and peas. Stir-fry for 2–3 minutes until the peas are cooked. Stir in the shrimp.

4 Roll up the omelets and roughly chop one-third of one, then slice the remainder into strips. Add the chopped omelet to the rice, peas and shrimp, and cook for 1–2 minutes until heated through. Divide the fried rice among four serving bowls, top with the sliced omelet and serve immediately.

Serves 4

Onions

1 Cut off the tip and bottom of the onion. Peel away all the layers of papery skin and any discolored layers underneath.

2 Put the onion root-end down on the cutting board, then, using a sharp knife, cut the onion in half from tip to bottom.

Slicing

Put one half on the board with the cut surface facing down and slice across the onion.

2

Chopping

Slice the halved onions from the root end to the top at regular intervals. Next, make two or three horizontal slices through the onion, then slice vertically across the width.

Seeding peppers

The seeds and white pith of bell peppers taste bitter, so should be removed.

1. Cut off the top of the pepper, then cut away and discard the seeds and white pith.
2. Alternatively, cut the pepper in half vertically and snap out the white pithy core and seeds. Trim away the rest of the white membrane with a small knife.

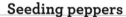

Rice and Red Pepper Stir-Fry

Prep time: 5 minutes
Cooking time: 15 minutes

scant ½ cup long-grain rice
¾ cup plus 2 tbsp. vegetable stock, hot
2 tsp. vegetable oil
½ onion, thinly sliced
2 bacon slices, chopped
1 small red bell pepper, seeded and
  cut into chunks
a handful of frozen peas
a dash of Worcestershire sauce

1 Put the rice in a pan and add the hot stock. Cover and bring to a boil, then reduce the heat and simmer for 10 minutes, or until the rice is tender and the liquid has been absorbed.

2 Meanwhile, heat the oil in a wok or large skillet over medium heat. Add the onion and fry for 5 minutes. Add the bacon and pepper and fry for 5 minutes longer, or until the bacon is crisp.

3 Stir the cooked rice and the peas into the onion mixture and cook, stirring occasionally, for 2–3 minutes until the rice and peas are hot. Add a dash of Worcestershire sauce and serve immediately.

Serves 4

Special Shrimp Fried Rice

Prep time: 5 minutes
Cooking time: about 13 minutes

1 tbsp. sesame oil
6 tbsp. nasi goreng paste
2¾ cups shredded green cabbage
9oz. (250g) cooked large, shelled
  shrimp
2½ cups microwaveable rice
2 tbsp. light soy sauce
1 tbsp. sunflower oil
2 eggs, beaten
2 scallions, thinly sliced
1 lime, cut into wedges, to serve

SAVE MONEY

If you prefer not to use
microwaveable rice, use
1 cup long-grain rice, cooked
according to the package
directions—but do not overcook.
Rinse the rice in cold water and
drain well before you begin
the recipe.

1 Heat the sesame oil in a wok
   and fry the nasi goreng paste for
   1–2 minutes. Add the cabbage and
   stir-fry for 2–3 minutes. Add the
   shrimp and stir briefly, then add
   the rice and soy sauce and cook
   for 5 minutes longer, stirring
   occasionally.

2 To make the omelet, heat the
   sunflower oil in a nonstick skillet
   (about 10in./25cm in diameter), then
   add the eggs. Swirl around to cover
   the bottom of the pan in a thin layer
   and cook for 2–3 minutes until set.

3 Roll up the omelet and cut it into
   strips. Serve the rice scattered with
   the omelet slices and scallions, and
   pass around the lime wedges to
   squeeze over each portion.

Serves 4

Yellow Bean Noodles with Jumbo Shrimp

Prep time: 10 minutes, plus soaking
Cooking time: 5 minutes

9oz. (250g) medium egg noodles

1 tbsp. vegetable oil or sesame oil

1 garlic clove, sliced

1 tsp. finely grated fresh ginger

1 bunch of scallions, each cut into four

9oz. (250g) raw shelled jumbo shrimp, thawed if frozen

2 bok choy, leaves separated and white stems cut into thick slices

¾ cup Chinese yellow bean stir-fry sauce

1 Put the noodles into a large heatproof bowl and cover with boiling water. Let soak for 4 minutes. Drain and set aside.

2 Heat the oil in a wok or large skillet. Add the garlic and ginger, then stir-fry for 30 seconds. Add the scallions and shrimp and continue stir-frying for 2 minutes longer.

3 Boil some water. Add the sliced white bok choy stems to the pan with the yellow bean sauce. Add the same amount of boiling water and stir well to mix.

4 Add the drained noodles to the pan and cook for 1 minute over high heat, tossing every now and then, until heated through. Stir in the bok choy leaves and serve immediately.

SAVE EFFORT

For an easy alternative, use chicken, cut into thin strips, instead of the shrimp.

Serves 4

Perfect Noodles

Noodles, along with rice, are one of the staples of Asian cooking. Often served as an accompaniment to stir-fried dishes, they can also be cooked separately and incorporated as one of the ingredients.

Cooking noodles:
Egg (wheat) noodles

These are the most versatile of Asian noodles. Like Italian pasta, they are made from wheat flour, egg, and water, and are available fresh or dried in a variety of thicknesses.

1 Bring a pot of water to a boil and add the noodles.
2 Agitate the noodles using chopsticks or a fork to separate them. This can take a minute or even longer.
3 Continue boiling for 4–5 minutes until the noodles are cooked al dente: tender but with a little bite in the middle.
4 Drain well and then rinse in cold water and toss with a little oil if you are not planning to use them immediately. This prevents them from sticking together.

Glass, cellophane, or bean thread noodles

These very thin noodles are made from mung beans; they need only 1 minute in boiling water.

Rice noodles

These can be very fine (rice vermicelli) or thick and flat. Most do not need cooking, only soaking in water. Check the package directions, or cover the noodles with freshly boiled water and soak them until they are al dente: tender but with a little bite in the middle. Drain well and toss with a little oil if you are not using them immediately. This prevents them from sticking together.

Perfect noodles

• Use 2–3oz. (50–75g) uncooked noodles per person.
• Dried egg noodles are often packed in layers. As a general rule, allow one layer per person for a main dish.
• If you plan to recook the noodles after the initial boiling or soaking—for example, in a stir-fry—it's best to undercook them slightly initially.
• When cooking a layer, block, or nest of noodles, use a pair of chopsticks or forks to untangle the strands from the moment the noodles go into the water.

Thai Noodles with Tofu

Prep time: 25 minutes
Cooking time: 35 minutes

4oz. (125g) firm tofu, drained and cut
　into 1in. (2.5cm) cubes
8 shallots, halved
1 garlic clove, crushed
1in. (2.5cm) piece of fresh ginger,
　peeled and grated
2 tbsp. soy sauce
1 tsp. rice vinegar
8oz. (225g) rice noodles
2 tbsp. unsalted peanuts
2 tbsp. sunflower oil
½ oz. (15g) dried shrimp (optional)
1 egg, beaten
¼ cup bean sprouts
fresh Thai basil leaves
　to garnish (optional)

For the sauce:

1 dried red chili, seeded and
　finely chopped
2 tbsp. lemon juice
1 tbsp. Thai fish sauce
1 tbsp. sugar
2 tbsp. smooth peanut butter

1 Heat the oven to 400°F (350°F for
convection ovens). Put the tofu and
shallots into a small roasting pan.
Put the garlic, ginger, soy sauce,
vinegar, and 2 tbsp. water in a bowl
and stir well. Pour the mixture over
the tofu and shallots and toss well
to coat. Roast near the top of the
oven for 30 minutes, or until the tofu
and shallots are golden.

2 Meanwhile, soak the noodles
according to the package directions.
Drain, refresh under cold running
water, and set aside. Toast and chop
the peanuts.

3 To make the sauce, put all the
ingredients in a small pan and
stir over low heat until the sugar
dissolves. Keep the sauce warm.

4 Heat the oil in a wok or large skillet
and stir-fry the dried shrimp,
if you like, for 1 minute. Add the
drained noodles and beaten egg to
the pan and stir-fry over medium
heat for 3 minutes. Add the tofu

Serves 4

and shallots, together with any pan juices. Stir well, then remove from the heat.

5 Stir in the bean sprouts and the sauce, then divide among four warm plates. Sprinkle with the toasted peanuts and serve immediately, garnished with Thai basil leaves, if you like.

Quick Pad Thai

Prep time: 12 minutes, plus soaking
Cooking time: 8 minutes

9oz. (250g) wide rice noodles

3 tbsp. satay sauce

1 tbsp. sweet chili sauce

1¼ cups thinly sliced snow peas

1¼ cups thinly sliced sugar snap peas

3 eggs, beaten

3 tbsp. chili soy sauce, plus extra
   to serve

9oz. (250g) cooked shelled
   jumbo shrimp

2 tbsp. roughly crushed dry-roasted
   peanuts

lime wedges to serve (optional)

SAVE EFFORT

Chili soy sauce can be replaced
with 2 tbsp. light soy sauce and
½ red chili, finely chopped (see
Safety Tip, page 28).

1 Put the noodles in a heatproof bowl, cover with boiling water, and soak for 4 minutes, or according to the package directions until softened. Drain, rinse under cold water and set aside.

2 Heat a wok or large skillet until hot. Add the satay and sweet chili sauces and stir-fry for 1 minute. Add the snow peas and sugar snap peas and cook for 2 minutes longer. Transfer to a bowl. Put the wok back on the heat, add the eggs, and stir-fry for 1 minute.

3 Add the soy sauce, shrimp, and noodles to the wok. Toss well and cook for 3 minutes until piping hot. Put the vegetables back into the pan, cook for 1 minute more until heated through, then sprinkle with the peanuts. Serve with extra soy sauce and lime wedges to squeeze over, if you like.

Serves 4

Pork and Noodle Stir-fry

Prep time: 15 minutes, plus marinating
Cooking time: about 8 minutes

1 tbsp. sesame oil

2in. (5cm) piece of fresh ginger, peeled
  and grated

2 tbsp. soy sauce

1 tbsp. Thai fish sauce

½ red chili, finely chopped (see Safety
  Tip, page 28)

1lb. (450g) pork tenderloin, cut into
  thin strips

2 red bell peppers, seeded and
  roughly chopped

9oz. (250g) baby corn cobs, halved
  lengthwise

2 cups halved sugar snap peas

3 cups bean sprouts

9oz. (250g) rice noodles

1 Put the oil in a large bowl. Add
  the ginger, soy sauce, fish sauce,
  chili, and pork strips. Mix well and
  marinate for 10 minutes.

2 Heat a wok or large skillet until hot.
  Lift the pork out of the marinade
  with a slotted spoon and add it to
  the pan. Stir-fry over high heat for
  5 minutes. Add the peppers, baby
  corn, sugar snap peas, bean sprouts,
  and remaining marinade and stir-fry
  for 2–3 minutes longer until the pork
  is cooked through.

3 Meanwhile, soak the noodles for
  4 minutes, or according to the
  package directions.

4 Drain the noodles, add them
  to the pan and toss well. Serve
  immediately.

Serves 4

Chicken Chow Mein

Prep time: 10 minutes
Cooking time: 10 minutes

9oz. (250g) medium egg noodles

1 tbsp. toasted sesame oil

2 boneless, skinless chicken breast
   halves, cut into thin strips

a bunch of scallions, thinly
   sliced diagonally

1½ cups sugar snap peas thickly sliced
   diagonally

1¼ cups bean sprouts

¾ cup thinly sliced cooked ham

½ cup chow mein sauce

salt and freshly ground black pepper

light soy sauce to serve

1 Cook the noodles in boiling water for 4 minutes, or according to the package directions. Drain, rinse thoroughly in cold water, and drain. Set aside.

2 Meanwhile, heat a wok or large skillet until hot. Add the oil and the chicken and stir-fry over high heat for 3–4 minutes until browned all over. Add the scallions and sugar snap peas and stir for 2 minutes, then stir in the bean sprouts and ham and stir-fry for 2 minutes.

3 Add the drained noodles, then pour the chow mein sauce over and toss together to coat evenly. Stir-fry for 2 minutes, or until piping hot. Season with salt and black pepper and serve immediately with light soy sauce to drizzle over.

Serves 4

Quick Chicken Stir-Fry

Hands-on time: 10 minutes
Cooking time: 12 minutes

1 tsp. groundnut oil

11oz. (300g) boneless, skinless chicken breast halves, sliced

4 scallions, chopped

7oz. (200g) medium rice noodles

1 cup sugar snap speas

200g (7oz) purple sprouting broccoli, chopped

2–3 tbsp. sweet chili sauce

cilantro leaves to garnish

lime wedges (optional) to serve

1 Heat the oil in a wok or large skillet. Add the chicken and scallions and stir-fry over a high heat for 5–6 minutes until the chicken is golden brown.

2 Meanwhile, soak the rice noodles in boiling water for 4 minutes or according to the pack instructions.

3 Add the sugar snap beas, broccoli, and chili sauce to the chicken. Continue to stir-fry for 4 minutes.

4 Drain the noodles, then add to the pan and toss everything together. Scatter the cilantro over the top and serve with lime wedges to squeeze over the stir-fry, if you like.

SAVE EFFORT

Other vegetables are just as good in this dish: try bok choy, button mushrooms, carrots cut into matchsticks, or baby sweetcorn.

Serves 4

Beef Chow Mein

Prep time: 15 minutes, plus marinating
Cooking time: 15 minutes

2 tsp. dark soy sauce

4 tsp. dry sherry

1 tsp. cornstarch

1 tsp. sugar

1 tbsp. sesame oil

8oz. (225g) boneless beef sirloin,
cut into thin strips about
3in. (7.5cm) long

6oz. (175g) egg noodles

3 tbsp. vegetable oil

1 bunch of scallions, sliced

3 garlic cloves, crushed

1 large green chili, sliced (see Safety
Tip, page 28)

1½ cups sliced Napa or green cabbage

½ cup bean sprouts

salt and freshly ground black pepper

1 Put the soy sauce, sherry, cornstarch, sugar, and 1 tsp. sesame oil in a bowl and whisk together. Pour this mixture over the beef. Cover and marinate in the refrigerator for at least 1 hour or overnight.

2 Cook the noodles for 4 minutes, or according to the package directions. Rinse under cold running water and drain.

3 Drain the beef, reserving the marinade. Heat the vegetable oil in a wok or large, nonstick skillet over high heat. Add the beef and stir-fry until well browned. Remove with a slotted spoon and set aside.

4 Add the scallions, garlic, chili, cabbage, and bean sprouts to the wok and stir-fry for 2–3 minutes. Put the beef back into the wok with the noodles and reserved marinade. Bring to a boil, stirring constantly, and cook for 2–3 minutes. Sprinkle the remaining sesame oil over, season, and serve immediately.

Serves 4

Mee Goreng

Prep time: 30 minutes
Cooking time: about 12 minutes

4oz. (125g) flank steak, very thinly
  sliced across the grain

2 garlic cloves

2 tbsp. soy sauce

1lb. (450g) cleaned squid

8oz. (225g) egg noodles

1 tbsp. vegetable oil

1 tbsp. sesame oil

1–2 hot red chilies, chopped (see Safety
  Tip, page 28)

1in. (2.5cm) piece of fresh ginger,
  peeled and finely chopped

2–3 scallions, sliced

6oz. (175g) raw large, shelled shrimp,
  deveined

2 tbsp. hoisin sauce

1 tbsp. lemon juice

2 tbsp. Thai fish sauce

1¼ cups bean sprouts

1 egg, beaten

lemon wedges to serve

1 Put the beef in a shallow dish with
  1 garlic clove and 1 tbsp. soy sauce.
  Let stand.

2 Wash and dry the squid. Cut the
  tentacles into small pieces. Open
  up the body pouches and cut into
  small rectangular pieces.

3 Put the noodles in a large heatproof
  bowl and cover with plenty
  of boiling water. Let soak for
  4 minutes, or according to the
  package directions.

4 Heat the vegetable and sesame
  oils in a wok or large skillet. Add
  the remaining garlic, the chilies,
  ginger, and scallions and stir-fry for
  2 minutes.

5 Add the beef and stir-fry for 2 minutes.
  Add the squid and shrimp and stir-fry
  for 2 minutes. Add the hoisin sauce,
  lemon juice, fish sauce, and remaining
  soy sauce and stir-fry for 2 minutes.

6 Drain the noodles and add them
  with the bean sprouts. Cook for
  2 minutes until heated through, then
  add the beaten egg. Cook briefly
  until the egg is on the point of
  setting. Serve with lemon wedges.

Serves 6

Veggie Dishes

Summer Vegetable Stir-Fry

Prep time: 15 minutes
Cooking time: about 8 minutes

4oz. (125g) baby carrots, scrubbed and trimmed

1 tbsp. sesame seeds

2 tbsp. sunflower oil

2 garlic cloves, roughly chopped

4oz. (125g) baby zucchini, halved lengthwise

1 large yellow bell pepper, seeded and cut into thick strips

4oz. (125g) thin asparagus spears, trimmed

4oz. (125g) cherry tomatoes, halved

salt and freshly ground black pepper

2 tbsp. balsamic or sherry vinegar

1 tsp. sesame oil

HEALTHY TIP

Vary the vegetables, but always blanch the harder ones first. For a winter vegetable stir-fry, use cauliflower and broccoli florets, carrot sticks, 2–3 sliced scallions, and a little chopped fresh ginger.

1 Blanch the baby carrots in boiling salted water for 2 minutes, then drain and pat dry.

2 Toast the sesame seeds in a hot dry wok or large skillet over medium heat, stirring until they turn golden. Transfer to a plate.

3 Put the wok or skillet back on the heat, add the sunflower oil, and heat until it is smoking. Add the garlic to the oil and stir-fry for 20 seconds. Add the carrots, zucchini, yellow pepper, and asparagus and stir-fry over high heat for 1 minute.

4 Add the cherry tomatoes and season to taste with salt and pepper. Stir-fry for 3–4 minutes until the vegetables are just tender. Add the vinegar and sesame oil, toss well, and sprinkle with the toasted sesame seeds. Serve immediately.

Serves 4

Sources of protein

Most vegetarians needn't worry about getting enough protein: this nutrient is found in a wide variety of foods, including beans, tofu and other soybean products, Quorn, eggs, cheese, and sprouted beans and seeds.

Legumes

This group encompasses all the various beans, peas, and lentils. They are highly nutritious, especially when eaten with grains, such as couscous, pasta, rice or bread. Dried legumes should be stored in airtight containers in a cool, dry cupboard. They keep well, but after about six months their skins start to toughen and they take progressively longer to cook. Most legumes must be soaked before cooking. Canned legumes are a convenient, quick alternative to having to soak and cook dried ones, and most supermarkets stock a wide range. A 15oz. (425g) can (drained weight about 8oz./225g) is roughly equivalent to ½ cup dried beans. Dried beans double in weight after soaking.

Sprouted beans and seeds

These are rich in nutrients and lend a nutty taste and crunchy texture to salads and stir-fries. Fresh bean sprouts are available from most supermarkets. Many beans and seeds can be sprouted at home, although it is important to buy ones that are specifically produced for sprouting—from a whole food store or other reliable source. Mung beans, aduki beans, alfalfa seeds, and fenugreek are all suitable.

Cheese

Some vegetarians prefer to avoid cheeses that have been produced by the traditional method, because they include animal-derived rennet. Many stores, however, now stock excellent ranges of vegetarian cheeses, produced using vegetarian rennet that comes from plants , such as thistle and mallow, which contain the enzynes capable of curdling milk.

Tofu

Also known as bean curd, tofu is made from ground soybeans in a process akin to cheese-making. It is highly nutritious, but virtually tasteless. However, it readily absorbs other flavors when marinated.

Tofu is a chilled product and should be stored in the refrigerator. Once opened, keep it immersed in a bowl of water in the refrigerator and eaten within four days.

Firm tofu is usually cut into chunks, then immersed in marinades or dressings prior to grilling, stir-frying, deep-frying, adding to stews, or adding to salads.

It can also be chopped and made into burgers and nut loaves. Smoked tofu has more flavor than unsmoked; it is used in the same way but doesn't need marinating. Silken tofu is softer and creamier than firm tofu and is useful for making sauces and dressings.

Textured vegetable protein (TVP)

TVP forms the bulk of most prepared vegetarian burgers, sausages, and ground products. It is made from a mixture of soy flour, flavorings, and liquid, which is cooked, then extruded under pressure and cut into chunks or small pieces to resemble ground meat. It has a slightly chewy, meat-like texture. TVP can be included in stews, pies, curries, and other dishes, rather as meat would be used by nonvegetarians.

Quorn™

Quorn is a vegetarian product derived from a distant relative of the mushroom. Although it is not suitable for vegans, because it contains egg albumen, Quorn is a good source of complete protein for vegetarians. Like tofu, Quorn has a bland flavor and benefits from being marinated before cooking. Find it in the refrigerator case at health food markets, and keep it in the refrigerator.

Sweet Chili and Tofu Stir-Fry

Prep time: 5 minutes, plus marinating
Cooking time: 12 minutes

7oz. (200g) firm tofu

4 tbsp. sweet chili sauce

2 tbsp. light soy sauce

1 tbsp. sesame seeds

2 tbsp. toasted sesame oil

heaped 3 cups prepared mixed stir-fry
    vegetables, such as carrots, broccoli,
    snow peas, and bean sprouts

a handful of pea shoots or baby salad
    greens to garnish

1 Drain the tofu, pat it dry, and cut it into large cubes. Put the tofu in a shallow container and pour 1 tbsp. sweet chili sauce and 1 tbsp. light soy sauce over. Cover and marinate for 10 minutes.

2 Meanwhile, toast the sesame seeds in a hot wok or large skillet until golden. Transfer to a plate.

3 Return the wok or skillet to the heat and add 1 tbsp. sesame oil. Add the marinated tofu and stir-fry for 5 minutes, or until golden. Remove and set aside.

4 Heat the remaining 1 tbsp. oil in the wok. Add the vegetables and stir-fry for 3–4 minutes until just tender. Stir in the cooked tofu.

5 Pour the remaining sweet chili sauce and soy sauce into the wok, toss well, and cook for 1 minute longer, or until heated through. Sprinkle with the sesame seeds and pea shoots and serve immediately.

Serves 4

Stir-Fried Vegetables with Oyster Sauce

Prep time: 20 minutes
Cooking time: about 10 minutes

6oz. (175g) firm tofu

vegetable oil to shallow- and
   deep-fry

2 garlic cloves, thinly sliced

1 green bell pepper, seeded and sliced

2½ cups broccoli cut into
   small florets

heaped 1 cup trimmed and halved
   green beans

2oz. (50g) bean sprouts

⅔ cup canned straw mushrooms,
   drained

¾ cup drained canned water chestnuts

fresh cilantro sprigs to garnish

For the sauce:

7 tbsp. vegetable stock

2 tbsp. vegetarian oyster sauce

1 tbsp. light soy sauce

2 tsp. honey

1 tsp. cornstarch

a pinch of salt

1 First, make the sauce. Put all the ingredients in a blender and blend until smooth. Set aside.

2 Drain the tofu, pat it dry, and cut it into large cubes. Heat the vegetable oil in a deep-fryer to 350°F. (Test by frying a small cube of bread; it should brown in 40 seconds.) Add the tofu and deep-fry for 1–2 minutes until golden. Drain on paper towels.

3 Heat 2 tbsp. oil in a wok or large skillet. Add the garlic and fry for 1 minute. Remove the garlic with a slotted spoon and discard. Add the pepper, broccoli, and beans to the oil in the wok and stir-fry for 3 minutes. Add the bean sprouts, mushrooms and water chestnuts and stir-fry for 1 minute longer.

4 Add the tofu and sauce to the wok and simmer, covered, for 3–4 minutes. Garnish with cilantro sprigs and serve immediately.

Serves 4

Tofu and Noodle Curry

Prep time: 15 minutes, plus marinating
Cooking time: about 25 minutes

9oz. (250g) firm tofu

2 tbsp. light soy sauce

½ red chili, chopped (see Safety Tip, page 28)

2in. (5cm) piece of fresh ginger, peeled and grated

1 tbsp. olive oil

1 onion, thinly sliced

2 tbsp. Thai red curry paste

¾ cup plus 2 tbsp. coconut milk

3¾ cups (900ml) vegetable stock, hot

7oz. (200g) baby corn cobs, halved lengthwise

7oz. (200g) green beans, trimmed

9oz. (250g) medium rice noodles

salt and freshly ground black pepper

2 scallions, sliced diagonally, fresh cilantro sprigs, and 1 lime, cut into wedges, to garnish

1 Drain the tofu, pat it dry, and cut it into large cubes. Put the tofu in a large shallow bowl with the soy sauce, chili, and ginger. Toss well to coat, then marinate for 30 minutes.

2 Heat the oil in a wok or large skillet. Add the onion and fry over medium heat for 10 minutes, stirring, until golden. Add the curry paste and cook for 2 minutes.

3 Add the marinated tofu, coconut milk, stock, and baby corn and season with salt and ground black pepper. Bring to a boil, then add the green beans. Reduce the heat and simmer for 8–10 minutes.

4 Meanwhile, put the noodles into a large heatproof bowl, add boiling water to cover, and soak for 30 seconds. Drain, then stir the noodles into the curry.

5 Pour the curry into four warm serving bowls and garnish with the scallions, cilantro, and lime wedges. Serve immediately.

Eggplant in a Hot Sweet-and-Sour Sauce

Prep time: 10 minutes
Cooking time: 35 minutes

3 tbsp. vegetable oil

1¼ cups thinly sliced onions

1in. (2.5cm) piece of fresh ginger,
peeled and finely chopped

2 red chilies, finely chopped, plus extra
whole red chilies (see Safety Tip,
page 28) to garnish (optional)

1½ tsp. cumin seeds

1½ tsp. coriander seeds

3 cloves

2in. (5cm) cinnamon stick

1 tbsp. paprika

juice of 2 limes

3-4 tbsp. dark muscovado
or brown sugar

1-2 tsp. salt

5⅔ cups eggplant cut into
1in. (2.5cm) pieces

boiled rice to serve

1 Heat the oil in a wok or large
skillet. Add the onions, ginger, and
chilies and stir-fry for about
4 minutes until softened. Add the
cumin and coriander seeds, cloves,
and cinnamon stick and cook for
2-3 minutes.

2 Add 1¼ cups (300ml) water to the
pan, then stir in the paprika, lime
juice, sugar, salt, and eggplant.
Bring to a boil, then reduce the heat
and simmer, covered, for 20 minutes,
or until the eggplant is tender.

3 Uncover the wok and bring the
sauce back to a boil. Boil for
3-4 minutes until the liquid is thick
enough to coat the eggplant pieces.
Serve with rice, garnished with
whole red chilies if you like.

Serves 4

Growing Your Own Sprouted Beans

Mung beans are the most commonly used sprouted beans for stir-fries, but chickpeas, green or Puy lentils, and alfalfa are equally good and easy for home sprouting.

Sprouting beans

You will only need about 3 tbsp. beans to sprout at one time.

1 Pick through the beans to remove any grit or stones, then soak in cold water for at least 8 hours. Drain and place in a clean (preferably sterilized) jar. Cover the top with a dampened piece of clean cloth, secure, and leave in a warm, dark place.

1

2 Rinse the sprouting beans twice a day. The sprouts can be eaten when there is about ½in. (1cm) of growth, or they can be left to grow for a day or two longer. When they are sprouted, leave the jar on a sunny windowsill for about 3 hours—this will improve both their flavor and their nutrients—then rinse and dry them well. They can be kept for about three days in the refrigerator.

HEALTHY TIPS

- Use only fresh bean sprouts; when buying, look for plump, crisp white shoots; avoid those that feel limp or are starting to brown.
- Store bean sprouts in a plastic bag in the refrigerator for up to two days.
- Rinse in ice-cold water and drain well before use.

2

Bean Sprouts with Peppers and Chilies

Prep time: 10 minutes
Cooking time: 5 minutes

3 tbsp. vegetable oil

2 garlic cloves, chopped

1in. (2.5cm) piece of fresh ginger, peeled and chopped

6 scallions, cut into 1in. (2.5cm) pieces

1 red bell pepper, seeded and thinly sliced

1 yellow bell pepper, seeded and thinly sliced

2 green chilies, seeded and finely chopped (see Safety Tip, page 28)

3½ cups bean sprouts

1 tbsp. dark soy sauce

1 tbsp. sugar

1 tbsp. vinegar

a few drops of sesame oil (optional)

boiled rice with 2 tbsp. chopped fresh cilantro stirred through to serve

1 Heat the oil in a wok or large skillet. Add the garlic, ginger, scallions, peppers, chilies, and bean sprouts and stir-fry over medium heat for 3 minutes.

2 Add the soy sauce, sugar, and vinegar and fry, stirring, for 1 minute longer.

3 Sprinkle with a few drops of sesame oil, if you like, then serve immediately with cilantro rice.

SAVE MONEY

Grow your own bean sprouts for this recipe following the technique on pages 106–107.

Egg Foo Yung

Prep time: 10 minutes
Cooking time: about 5 minutes

3 tbsp. peanut or vegetable oil

8 scallions, thinly sliced, plus scallion curls (see Try This, page 144) to garnish

1¾ cups sliced shiitake or oyster mushrooms

½ cup chopped canned bamboo shoots, drained

½ green bell pepper, seeded and finely chopped

scant 1 cup frozen peas, thawed

6 eggs, beaten

pinch of cayenne pepper,

1 tbsp. light soy sauce

a pinch of salt

1 Heat the oil in a wok or large skillet. Add the scallions, mushrooms, bamboo shoots, green pepper, and peas and stir-fry for 2–3 minutes.

2 Season the eggs with salt and cayenne. Pour the eggs into the pan and continue to cook, stirring, until the egg mixture is set.

3 Sprinkle the soy sauce over the eggs and stir well. Serve immediately, garnished with scallion curls.

Vegetable Fried Rice

1 cup long-grain rice

3 Chinese dried mushrooms, or
   1¾ cups sliced button mushrooms,

2 tbsp. vegetable oil

4 scallions, sliced diagonally
   into 1in. (2.5cm) lengths

¾ cup canned bamboo shoots, drained
   and cut into 1in (2.5cm) strips

4 cups bean sprouts

scant 1 cup frozen peas

2 tbsp. soy sauce

3 eggs, beaten

fresh cilantro sprigs to garnish

1 Put the rice in a pan, cover with enough cold water to come 1in. (2.5cm) above the rice, and bring to a boil. Cover tightly, reduce the heat, and simmer very gently for 20 minutes. Do not stir.

2 Remove the pan from the heat, let cool for 20 minutes, then cover with plastic wrap and chill for 2–3 hours or overnight.

3 When ready to fry the rice, soak the dried mushrooms, if using, in warm water for about 30 minutes.

4 Drain the mushrooms, squeeze out excess moisture, then thinly slice.

5 Heat the oil in a wok or large skillet over high heat. Add the mushrooms, scallions, bamboo shoots, bean sprouts, and peas and stir-fry for 2–3 minutes. Add the soy sauce and cook briefly, stirring.

6 Fluff the cold rice with a fork, add it to the pan, and stir-fry for 2 minutes. Pour in the eggs and continue to stir-fry for 2–3 minutes until the egg has scrambled and the rice is heated through. Serve immediately, garnished with cilantro.

Serves 4

Crispy Noodles with Hot Sweet-and-Sour Sauce

Prep time: 10 minutes
Cooking time: about 15 minutes

vegetable oil to deep-fry

heaped ½ cup rice or 4oz. (125 g) egg noodles

frisée lettuce for serving

For the sauce:

2 tbsp. vegetable oil

1 garlic clove, crushed

½in. (1cm) piece of fresh ginger, peeled and grated

6 scallions, sliced

½ red bell pepper, seeded and finely chopped

2 tbsp. sugar

2 tbsp. vinegar

2 tbsp. ketchup

2 tbsp. dark soy sauce

2 tbsp. dry sherry

1 tbsp. cornstarch

1 tbsp. sliced green chilies (see Safety Tip, page 28)

1 First, make the sauce. Heat the oil in a wok or large skillet. Add the garlic, ginger, scallions, and red pepper and stir-fry for 1 minute. Stir in the sugar, vinegar, ketchup, soy sauce, and sherry. Blend the cornstarch with ½ cup (125ml) water and stir it into the sauce. Cook for 2 minutes, stirring. Add the chilies, cover, and keep the sauce warm.

2 Heat the vegetable oil in a deep-fryer to 375°F. (Test by frying a small cube of bread; it should brown in 20 seconds.) Cut the noodles into six portions and fry, a batch at a time, quickly until lightly golden. Take care as the hot oil rises up quickly.

3 Drain the noodles on paper towels and keep them warm while you cook the remainder.

4 Arrange the noodles on a bed of frisée and serve immediately with the sauce served on the side.

Serves 4

Fish and Seafood

Chili and Crab Noodles

Prep time: 10 minutes
Cooking time: about 15 minutes

7oz. (200g) medium egg noodles

1 tbsp. vegetable oil

scant 3 cups frozen mixed vegetables

6 tbsp. sweet chili sauce

1 tbsp. soy sauce

½ tbsp. cornstarch

7 tbsp. chicken or vegetable stock

1 cup drained canned crab

frozen or chopped fresh cilantro leaves
  (optional)

1 Bring a pot of water to a boil and cook the noodles according to the package directions. Drain well and set aside.

2 Heat the oil in a large wok until smoking. Add the mixed vegetables and stir-fry for 5 minutes, or until piping hot.

3 In a small bowl, stir together the sweet chili sauce, soy sauce, cornstarch, and stock. Add the sauce to the wok; boil for 1 minute, then toss with the noodles, crab and cilantro, if you like. Check the seasoning and serve immediately.

TRY THIS

If you don't have canned crab, any canned fish or fresh or thawed seafood will work here.

Serves 4

Perfect Scallops

Scallops are a delicately flavored shellfish, contained within shells
that can be a little tricky to open. Ask your fish merchant to prepare them
if you prefer. The scallops themselves have a marvelous taste.

Opening scallops

Scallops can be eaten raw, either
seasoned or marinated in citrus
juice with seasonings. They take
very little cooking, usually between
5 and 10 minutes.

1   Hold the scallop with the flat
    half of the shell facing up. Firmly
    ease a very sharp, small knife
    between the shells at a point
    close to the hinge.

1

2 Keeping the knife angled toward the flat shell, cut all along the shell surface until the two shells can be separated easily. Cut along the bottom of the rounded shell to release its contents. Cut loose the meat and the gray/orange roe and discard everything else.

3 Rinse off any grit, cut the roe from the round meat, and cut the little scrap of muscle from the edge of the meat.

Cooking scallops

• Gently poach the white meat in wine for 5 minutes, then add the roe and simmer for 5 minutes.

• Sauté until crisp on the outside.

• Sear briefly on each side in a very hot pan until the surface browns and the inside remains tender.

• Thread onto skewers and broil.

• Bake in the shell with a sauce.

2

Scallops with Ginger

Prep time: 15 minutes
Cooking time: 3 minutes

2 tbsp. vegetable oil

1lb. 2oz. (500g) shelled large scallops, cut into ¼in. (0.5cm) slices

4 celery ribs, sliced diagonally

1 bunch of scallions, sliced diagonally

1oz. (25g) piece of fresh ginger, peeled and sliced

2 large garlic cloves, sliced

¼ tsp. cayenne pepper, or to taste

2 tbsp. lemon juice

2 tbsp. light soy sauce

3 tbsp. chopped fresh cilantro

salt and freshly ground black pepper

1 Heat the oil in a wok or large skillet. Add the scallops, celery, scallions, ginger, garlic, and cayenne and stir-fry over high heat for 2 minutes or until the vegetables are just tender.

2 Pour in the lemon juice and soy sauce and let bubble up, then stir in about 2 tbsp. chopped cilantro and season with salt and ground black pepper. Serve immediately sprinkled with the remaining chopped cilantro.

Serves 4

Perfect Mussels

One of the most popular shellfish, mussels take moments to cook.
Careful preparation is important, so give yourself enough time
to get the shellfish ready.

Preparing mussels

1 Scrape off the fibers attached to the shells (beards). If the mussels are very clean, give them a quick rinse under cold water. If they are very sandy, scrub them with a stiff brush.

2 If the shells have sizeable barnacles on them, it is best (although not essential) to remove them. Rap them sharply with a metal spoon or the back of a scrub brush, then scrape off.

1

Cooking mussels

1. Discard any open mussels that don't shut when sharply tapped; this means they are dead and can be dangerous to eat.

2. In a large, heavy pan, fry 2 finely chopped shallots and a generous handful of parsley in 2 tbsp. butter for about 2 minutes or until soft. Pour in ½in. (1cm) dry white wine.

3. Add the mussels to the pan and cover tightly with a lid. Steam for 5–10 minutes until the shells open. Immediately take the pan off the heat.

4. Using a slotted spoon, remove the mussels from the pan and discard any that haven't opened, then boil the cooking liquid rapidly to reduce. Pour over the mussels and serve immediately.

2

3

Thai Coconut Mussels

Prep time: 15 minutes
Cooking time: about 12 minutes

1 tbsp. vegetable oil
2 shallots, finely chopped
2–3 tbsp. Thai green curry paste
1¾ cups coconut milk
4½lb. (2kg) mussels, scrubbed and
   beards removed
a small handful of fresh cilantro,
   chopped, plus extra sprigs
   to garnish

1 Heat the oil in a large, deep pan.
  Add the shallots and curry paste
  and fry gently for 5 minutes, stirring
  regularly, or until the shallots are
  starting to soften. Stir in the coconut
  milk, cover with a tight-fitting lid
  and bring to a boil.

2 Add the mussels to the pan, cover,
  shake the pan well, and cook over
  medium heat for 4–5 minutes. Give
  the pan another good shake. Check
  the mussels and discard any that
  are still closed. Stir in the chopped
  cilantro and serve immediately,
  garnished with cilantro sprigs.

TRY THIS

For an easy alternative, instead
of mussels you can use 1lb. 2oz.
(500g) raw large, shelled shrimp;
simmer for 5 minutes, or until the
shrimp are cooked and pink.

Serves 4

Perfect Shrimp

Like mussels and small squid, shrimp are ideal for stir-frying and quick braising, because they need very brief cooking. If they are overcooked they will become rubbery in texture.

Shelling and butterflying

1. To shell shrimp, pull off the head and set aside. Using pointed scissors, cut through the soft shell on the belly side.

2. Pull the shell off, leaving the tail attached. (Add to the head; it can be used later for making stock.)

3. Using a small sharp knife, make a shallow cut along the length of the back of the shrimp. Use

the point of the knife to carefully remove and discard the black vein (intestinal tract) that runs along the back of the shrimp.

4 To "butterfly" the shrimp, cut halfway through the flesh lengthwise from the head end to the base of the tail, and open up the shrimp.

Langoustines and crayfish

Related to the shrimp, langoustines and crayfish can be peeled in the same way as shrimp. To extract the meat from langoustine claws, pull off the small pincer from the claws, then work with small scissors to cut open the main section all the way along its length. Split open and carefully pull out the flesh in a single piece. To extract the meat from large crayfish claws, crack them open using a hammer or lobster cracker, then carefully remove the meat.

Also called Dublin Bay prawns, langoustines are at their best when just boiled or steamed, and then eaten from the shells. They can also be used in a shellfish soup.

Crayfish are sold either live or cooked. To cook, boil in court bouillon for 5–10 minutes. Remove from the stock and cool. Eat crayfish from the shell or in a soup.

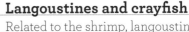

Shrimp and Cucumber in a Spicy Sauce

Prep time: 20 minutes, plus standing
Cooking time: about 30 minutes

2 cucumbers, halved lengthwise, seeded, and cut into 1in. (2.5cm) chunks

4 tbsp. butter

2 onions, sliced

2 garlic cloves, finely chopped

4 tsp. all-purpose flour

2 tsp. ground turmeric

1 tsp. ground cinnamon

2 tsp. sugar

½ tsp. ground cloves

3 cups (750ml) coconut milk

1¼ cups (300ml) fish stock

1 tbsp. peeled and thinly sliced ginger

3-4 green chilies, thinly sliced (see Safety Tip, page 28)

1lb. (450g) raw jumbo shrimp, shelled and deveined

grated zest and juice of 1 lime

2 tbsp. freshly chopped cilantro

salt

SAVE TIME

If raw shrimp are difficult to find, use cooked ones instead. Add them to the sauce and heat through for 2–3 minutes—no longer or they will become rubbery.

1 Put the cucumber in a colander set over a bowl and sprinkle with salt. Leave for 30 minutes, to let the salt extract the excess juices.

2 Melt the butter in a pan. Add the onions and garlic and cook for about 5 minutes until softened. Add the flour, turmeric, cinnamon, 1 tsp. salt, the sugar, and cloves; cook, stirring, for 2 minutes. Add the coconut milk and stock, bring to a boil, reduce the heat and simmer for 5 minutes.

Serves 4

3 Meanwhile, rinse the cucumber thoroughly under cold running water to remove the salt. Add the cucumber, ginger, and chilies to the sauce, and cook for 10 minutes longer.

4 Add the shrimp to the sauce and cook for another 5–6 minutes until they turn pink.

5 Just before serving, stir in the lime juice and chopped cilantro and sprinkle with lime zest.

Stir-Fried Shrimp with Cabbage

Prep time: 30 minutes
Cooking time: about 7 minutes

2 tbsp. vegetable oil

2 garlic cloves, thinly sliced

1 lemongrass stalk, halved and bruised

2 kaffir lime leaves, finely torn

1 small red onion, thinly sliced

1 hot red chili, seeded and sliced (see
   Safety Tip, page 28)

1½in. (4cm) piece of fresh ginger,
   peeled and cut into long thin shreds

1 tbsp. coriander seeds, lightly crushed

1lb. (450g) raw large, shelled shrimp,
   deveined

1¾ cups halved snow peas

8oz. (225g) bok choy or Chinese
   mustard cabbage, torn into
   bite-size pieces

2 tbsp. Thai fish sauce

juice of 1 lime, or to taste

1 Heat the oil in a wok or large skillet.
Add the garlic, lemongrass, lime
leaves, onion, chili, ginger,
and coriander seeds and stir-fry
for 2 minutes.

2 Add the shrimp, snow peas, and bok
choy or cabbage, and stir-fry until
the vegetables are cooked but still
crisp and the shrimp are pink and
opaque—2–3 minutes.

3 Add the fish sauce and lime juice
and cook for 1 minute until heated
through. Remove the lemongrass
and discard; serve immediately.

HEALTHY TIP

Chinese mustard cabbage,
otherwise called mustard greens,
is a green or red Asian leaf that
has a mild mustard flavor.

Five-Minute Stir-Fry

Prep time: 2 minutes
Cooking time: 5 minutes

1 tbsp. sesame oil

6oz. (175g) raw shelled jumbo shrimp, deveined

¼ cup bought sweet chili and ginger sauce

1¾ cups prepared mixed stir-fry vegetables, such as sliced zucchini, broccoli, and green beans

1 Heat the oil in a large wok or skillet. Add the shrimp and sweet chili and ginger sauce and stir-fry for 2 minutes.

2 Add the mixed vegetables and stir-fry for another 2–3 minutes until the shrimp are cooked and the vegetables are heated through. Serve immediately.

TRY THIS

For an easy variation, instead of shrimp, try chicken cut into strips; stir-fry for 5 minutes in step 1.

Serves 2

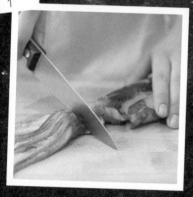

1

Preparing squid

Sliced into rings or cut into squares, squid is popular in Chinese and Southeast Asian cooking.

1 Cut off the tentacles just behind the "beak."
2 Pull out the beak and discard. Clean the tentacles well, scraping off as many of the small suckers as you can.
3 Reach inside the body and pull out the internal organs, including the plastic-like "pen."

2

3

4 Scrape and pull off the loose, slippery skin covering the body. Rinse the body thoroughly to remove all internal organs, sand and other debris.

5 Detach the wings and set aside, then cut up the tentacles and body as required. To make squares, slice the body along one side, then score diagonally and cut into squares.

4

5

Squid and Vegetables in Black Bean Sauce

Prep time: 35 minutes
Cooking time: about 15 minutes

1lb. (450g) cleaned squid

2 tbsp. sesame seeds

2 tbsp. sunflower oil

1 tbsp. sesame oil

2 garlic cloves

2 dried red chilies

½ cup broccoli florets

½ cup trimmed snow peas

½ cup thinly sliced carrots

⅔ cup cauliflower cut into small florets (optional)

1 small green or red bell pepper, seeded and thinly sliced

⅔ cup shredded Napa cabbage or bok choy

1oz. (25g) bean sprouts

2 tbsp. fresh cilantro, roughly torn

TRY THIS

Instead of squid, use 14oz. (400g) beef sirloin, cut into thin strips.

For the sauce:

2 tbsp. black bean sauce

1 tbsp. Thai fish sauce

2–3 tsp. honey

5 tbsp. fish or vegetable stock

1 tbsp. tamarind juice

2 tsp. cornstarch

1 First, prepare the sauce. In a small bowl, mix together the black bean sauce, fish sauce, honey, and stock. Add the tamarind juice and cornstarch and whisk until smooth. Set aside.

2 Wash and dry the squid, and halve the tentacles if large. Open up the body pouches and score diagonally, then cut into large squares; set aside.

3 Toast the sesame seeds in a dry wok or large skillet over medium heat, stirring until they turn golden. Transfer to a plate.

Serves 4

4 Heat the sunflower and sesame oils in the same pan. Add the garlic and chilies and fry slowly for 5 minutes. Remove the garlic and chilies with a slotted spoon and discard.

5 Add all the vegetables to the pan and stir-fry for 3 minutes. Add the squid, increase the heat, and stir-fry for 2 minutes longer, or until the squid curls and turns opaque. Add the sauce and simmer for 1 minute.

6 Scatter the sesame seeds and cilantro over and serve immediately.

Stir-Fried Salmon and Broccoli

Prep time: 10 minutes
Cooking time: about 6 minutes

2 tsp. sesame oil

1 red bell pepper, seeded and thinly sliced

½ red chili, thinly sliced (see Safety Tip, page 28)

1 garlic clove, crushed

1¼ cups small broccoli florets

2 scallions, sliced

2 salmon fillets, about 4oz. (125g) each, cut into strips

1 tsp. Thai fish sauce

2 tsp. soy sauce

soba noodles to serve

1 Heat the oil in a wok or large skillet and add the red pepper, chili, garlic, broccoli florets, and scallions. Stir-fry over high heat for 3–4 minutes.

2 Add the salmon, fish sauce, and soy sauce and cook for 2 minutes, stirring gently. Serve immediately with soba noodles.

Serves 2

Perfect Steaming

To use your wok as a steamer you will need a trivet or steamer rack to place inside the wok. The steamer basket (metal or bamboo) sits on the trivet to keep the food above a boiling liquid. Steaming is ideal for fish, chicken, and most vegetables.

1. Put the fish or chicken on a lightly greased heatproof plate that will fit inside the steamer. (Vegetables can be placed directly on the steamer.)
2. Bring the water in the wok or pan to a boil over medium heat. Put the plate with the fish or chicken in the steamer, cover with a tight-fitting lid, and steam until just cooked through (see chart, right).

HEALTHY TIP

Steaming allows food to retain maximum flavor and color, as well as the vitamins that are easily lost during boiling or poaching.

STEAMING TIMES

Leafy vegetables, such as spinach, Chinese greens	1–2 minutes
Vegetables, such as green beans, broccoli, cauliflower, cabbage, carrots	5–8 minutes
Fish fillets	5–10 minutes (allow 10 minutes per 1in. (2.5cm) thickness)
Fish steaks and whole fish	15–20 minutes
Chicken	45–50 minutes (depending on whether chicken is shredded, cubed, boned thighs, or breast halves)

Steamed Sesame Salmon

Prep time: 20 minutes
Cooking time: about 18 minutes

peanut or vegetable oil to brush

8–12 large Napa cabbage or lettuce leaves

4 salmon steaks, about 5oz. (150g) each

½ tsp. sesame oil

2 tbsp. dry sherry

2 tbsp. light soy sauce, plus extra to serve

4 scallions, shredded, plus extra scallion curls to garnish

1 tbsp. sesame seeds, lightly toasted in a dry wok or heavy pan

ground white pepper

TRY THIS

To make perfect scallion curls, trim scallions into 3in. (7.5cm) lengths, then shred finely. Place in a bowl of water with ice cubes for 30 minutes.

1 Steam the cabbage leaves or lettuce leaves for 1–2 minutes until soft and pliable. Discard about 1in. (2.5cm) of the firm stem end from each leaf to neaten, and place 2–3 leaves together, slightly overlapping. Put the salmon steaks on top.

2 Mix the sesame oil with the sherry and soy sauce and drizzle the mixture over the salmon. Sprinkle with the shredded scallions, 2 tsp. sesame seeds and ground white pepper to taste.

3 Fold the leaves over the salmon to form neat bundles. Steam for 5–7 minutes until the fish is cooked and flakes easily.

4 Serve the salmon bundles with the juices spooned over. Sprinkle with the remaining sesame seeds and a little extra soy sauce, then garnish with scallion curls.

Serves 4

Teriyaki Salmon with Spinach

Prep time: 10 minutes, plus marinating
Cooking time: 6 minutes

1¼lb. (550g) salmon fillet,
   cut into ½in. (1cm) slices
3 tbsp. teriyaki sauce
3 tbsp. tamari or light soy sauce
2 tbsp. vegetable oil
1 tbsp. sesame oil
1 tbsp. chopped fresh chives
2 tsp. grated fresh ginger
2 garlic cloves, crushed
12oz. (350g) soba noodles
12oz. (350g) baby spinach leaves
furikake seasoning

1 Gently mix the salmon slices with
  the teriyaki sauce, then cover, chill.
  and marinate for 1 hour.
2 Mix together the tamari, 1 tbsp.
  vegetable oil, sesame oil, chives,
  ginger, and garlic. Set aside.
3 Cook the noodles according to
  the package directions. Drain and
  set aside.
4 Heat the remaining vegetable oil in
  a wok or large skillet. Remove the
  salmon from the marinade and add
  it to the wok. Cook over high heat
  until it turns opaque—about
  30 seconds. Remove from the wok
  and set aside.
5 Add the drained noodles to the
  wok and stir until warm through.
  Stir in the spinach and cook for
  1–2 minutes until wilted. Add the soy
  sauce mixture and stir to combine.

HEALTHY TIPS

Furikake seasoning is a Japanese
condiment made of sesame seeds
and chopped seaweed. It can be
found in major supermarkets and
Asian food stores.
   Soba noodles are made from
buckwheat and are gluten-free.
If you have a wheat allergy or
gluten intolerance, look for 100%
soba on the pack.

Serves 4

6 Divide the noodles among four
   warm, deep bowls, then top with
   the salmon. Sprinkle with furikake
   seasoning and serve.

Hearty Dishes

Stir-Frying Poultry and Meat

Stir-frying is a healthy and speedy way to cook poultry and other tender cuts of meat.

Preparing and cooking

1 Trim off any fat, then cut the poultry or meat into even-size strips or dice no more than ¼in. (0.5cm) thick. Heat a wok or large pan until hot and add oil to coat the inside.

2 Add the poultry or meat and cook, stirring constantly, until just done. Remove and set aside. Cook the other ingredients you are using for the stir-fry, then put the poultry or meat back into the pan and cook for 1–2 minutes to heat through.

HEALTHY TIP

Stir-frying in a wok uses less fat than other frying techniques, and cooking quickly over high heat retains as many nutrients as possible.

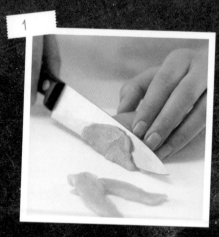

Slicing boneless breasts

1 Cut or pull out the long strip of flesh lying on the inside of the breast. Slice the meat across the grain to the thickness required for your recipe. (Raw chicken should not be cut less than about ⅛in./0.3cm thick.)
2 Starting at the small tip of the breast, cut slices of the required thickness. Alternatively, cut into chunks or dice.

Perfect slicing

To make slicing easier, put boneless breast halves in the freezer for 30 minutes or so before slicing. The flesh will be much firmer and it will, therefore, be easier to slice it thinly.

2

Pork Stir-Fry with Chili and Mango

Prep time: 5 minutes
Cooking time: about 10 minutes

3oz. (75g) medium egg noodles

1 tsp. peanut oil

½ red chili, seeded and finely chopped
(see Safety Tip, page 28)

4oz. (125g) pork tenderloin, cut into
thin strips

1 head bok choy, roughly chopped

1 tbsp. soy sauce

½ ripe mango, sliced

1 Bring a large pot of water to a boil. Add the noodles and cook for 4 minutes, or according to the package directions. Drain, then plunge into cold water. Set aside.

2 Meanwhile, heat the oil in a wok or large skillet until very hot. Add the chili and pork and stir-fry for 3-4 minutes. Add the bok choy and soy sauce and stir-fry for 2-3 minutes longer. Add the mango and toss to combine.

3 Drain the noodles and add them to the pan. Toss well and stir for 1-2 minutes until heated through. Serve immediately.

Serves 2

Sweet-and-Sour Pork Stir-Fry

Prep time: 15 minutes
Cooking time: about 10 minutes

2 tbsp. vegetable oil

12oz. (350g) pork tenderloin, cut into thin strips

1 red onion, thinly sliced

1 red bell pepper, seeded and thinly sliced

2 carrots, cut into thin strips

3 tbsp. sweet chili sauce

1 tbsp. white wine vinegar

½ cup chopped canned pineapple slices, with 2 tbsp. juice reserved

a large handful of bean sprouts

½ tbsp. sesame seeds

a large handful of fresh cilantro, roughly chopped

salt and freshly ground black pepper

boiled long-grain rice to serve

1 Heat the oil over high heat in a large wok or skillet. Add the pork, onion, red pepper, and carrots and stir-fry for 3–5 minutes until the meat is cooked through and the vegetables are softening.

2 Stir in the chili sauce, vinegar, and reserved pineapple juice and bring to a boil, then stir in the pineapple chunks and bean sprouts and cook until heated through.

3 Check the seasoning. Scatter the sesame seeds and cilantro over and serve immediately with rice.

SAVE TIME

As with all stir-fries, have everything sliced and ready before you start cooking.

Serves 4

Turkey and Sesame Stir-Fry with Noodles

Prep time: 5 minutes, plus 5 minutes marinating
Cooking time: 10 minutes

11oz. (300g) boneless turkey breast meat, cut into thin strips

3 tbsp. teriyaki marinade

3 tbsp. honey

1lb. 2oz. (500g) medium egg noodles

about 1 tbsp. sesame oil, plus extra for the noodles

11oz. (300g) prepared mixed stir-fry vegetables, such as carrots, broccoli, red cabbage, snow peas, bean sprouts, and scallions

2 tbsp. sesame seeds, lightly toasted in a dry wok or heavy pan

1 Put the turkey strips in a large bowl with the teriyaki marinade and honey and stir to coat. Cover and set aside for 5 minutes.

2 Bring a large pot of water to a boil. Add the noodles and cook for 4 minutes, or according to the package directions. Drain well, then toss with a little sesame oil.

3 Heat 1 tbsp. of the oil in a wok or large skillet. Add the turkey, reserving the marinade, and stir-fry over very high heat for 2–3 minutes until cooked through and beginning to brown. Add a drop more oil, if needed, then add the vegetables and reserved marinade. Continue to stir-fry over high heat until the vegetables have started to soften and the sauce is warm through.

4 Scatter with the sesame seeds and serve immediately with the noodles.

Serves 4

Orange and Ginger Beef Stir-Fry

Prep time: 15 minutes
Cooking time: about 8 minutes

1 tbsp. cornstarch

5 tbsp. orange juice, pulp free

2 tbsp. soy sauce

1 tbsp. vegetable oil

14oz. (400g) tender beef, cut into strips

2in. (5cm) piece of fresh ginger, peeled and cut into matchsticks

2 cups mixed stir-fry vegetables of your choice, chopped if large

salt and freshly ground black pepper

1 tbsp. sesame seeds

boiled egg noodles to serve

1 Put the cornstarch into a small bowl and gradually whisk in the orange juice followed by the soy sauce to make a smooth mixture. Set aside.

2 Heat the oil over high heat in a large skillet or wok. Add the beef strips and stir-fry for 1–2 minutes. Stir in the ginger, vegetables, and a splash of water and stir-fry until the vegetables are just tender and the beef is cooked to your liking.

3 Add the orange juice mixture to the wok and stir-fry until thick and syrupy—about 30 seconds. Season to taste with salt and black pepper and sprinkle the sesame seeds over. Serve immediately with boiled egg noodles.

Serves 4

Sichuan Beef

12oz. (350g) skirt or flank steak, cut into thin strips

5 tbsp. hoisin sauce

4 tbsp. dry sherry

2 tbsp. vegetable oil

2 red or green chilies, finely chopped (see Safety Tip, page 28)

1 large onion, thinly sliced

2 garlic cloves, crushed

2 red bell peppers, seeded and cut into diamond shapes

1in. (2.5cm) piece of fresh ginger, peeled and grated

1¾ cups drained and sliced canned bamboo shoots

1 tbsp. sesame oil

1 Put the beef in a bowl, add the hoisin sauce and sherry, and stir to coat. Cover and marinate for 30 minutes.

2 Heat the vegetable oil in a wok or large skillet until smoking hot. Add the chilies, onion, and garlic and stir-fry over medium heat for 3–4 minutes until softened. Remove with a slotted spoon and set aside. Add the red peppers, increase the heat, and stir-fry for a few seconds. Remove from the pan and set aside.

3 Add the steak and marinade to the wok in batches. Stir-fry each batch over high heat for about 1 minute, removing with a slotted spoon.

4 Put the vegetables back into the pan. Add the ginger and bamboo shoots, then the beef, and stir-fry for 1 minute longer, or until heated through. Transfer to a warm serving dish, sprinkle the sesame oil over the top and serve immediately.

Teriyaki Beef Stir-Fry

Prep time: 20 minutes, plus marinating
Cooking time: about 8 minutes

1lb. (450g) beef tenderloin, sliced as
   thinly as possible, then cut into
   ½in.- (1cm)-wide strips
2 tbsp. vegetable or peanut oil
1½ cups carrots cut into matchsticks
½ cucumber, seeded and cut into
   matchsticks
4–6 scallions, thinly sliced diagonally
noodles tossed in a little sesame oil
   and wasabi paste (optional) to serve

For the teriyaki marinade:

4 tbsp. tamari
4 tbsp. mirin or medium sherry
1 garlic clove, finely chopped
1in. (2.5cm) piece of fresh ginger,
   peeled and finely chopped

1 First, make the marinade. Put all
the ingredients for the marinade
in a shallow bowl and mix well. Add
the beef and turn to coat. Cover and
marinate in the refrigerator for at
least 30 minutes, or overnight.

2 Drain the beef, reserving any
marinade to one side. Heat a wok
or large skillet. Add the oil and heat
until it is smoking. Add the carrots,
cucumber, and scallions and stir-fry
over high heat for 2 minutes until
the edges are well browned. Remove
from the pan and set aside.

3 Add the beef to the wok and stir-fry
over very high heat for 2 minutes.

4 Put the vegetables back into the
wok and add the reserved marinade.
Stir-fry for 1–2 minutes until heated
through. Serve with noodles tossed
in a little sesame oil and a small
amount of wasabi paste if you like.

Serves 4

Quick Turkey and Pork Stir-Fry

Prep time: 15 minutes
Cooking time: about 10 minutes

1 tbsp. vegetable oil

1⅓ cups turkey breast meat cut into thin strips

1⅓ cups pork tenderloin cut into thin strips

1 tbsp. Chinese 5-spice powder

1 each yellow and orange bell pepper, seeded and sliced

2 cups thickly shredded bok choy

1 tsp. sesame seeds

1–1½ tbsp. soy sauce, to taste

a large handful of fresh cilantro

salt and freshly ground black pepper

1 Heat the oil in a large wok or skillet over high heat. Add the turkey and pork and cook for 3 minutes, stirring occasionally. Add the Chinese 5-spice powder, the sliced peppers, bok choy, and a splash of water.

2 Continue to cook for a few minutes until the vegetables are tender and the meat is cooked through. (Add more water as needed.)

3 Sprinkle the sesame seeds over, add the soy sauce, and top with the cilantro. Season to taste with salt and pepper and serve with noodles or rice if you like.

TRY THIS

If you prefer not to mix the two meats, then simply make up the quantity using one or the other.

Chicken with Peanut Sauce

Prep time: 10 minutes, plus marinating
Cooking time: about 10 minutes

4 boneless, skinless chicken breast
 halves, cut into strips
1 tbsp. ground coriander
2 garlic cloves, finely chopped
4 tbsp. vegetable oil
2 tbsp. honey
Thai fragrant rice to serve
fresh cilantro sprigs to garnish

For the peanut sauce:

1 tbsp. vegetable oil
2 tbsp. curry paste
2 tbsp. brown sugar
2 tbsp. peanut butter
¾ cup plus 2 tbsp. coconut milk

1 Mix the chicken with the ground
 coriander, garlic, oil, and honey.
 Cover and marinate in the
 refrigerator for 15 minutes.
2 To make the peanut sauce, heat
 the oil in a pan. Add the curry paste,
 brown sugar, and peanut butter and
 fry for 1 minute. Add the coconut
 milk and bring to a boil, stirring
 constantly, then reduce the heat and
 simmer for 5 minutes.
3 Meanwhile, heat a wok or large
 skillet. When hot, add the chicken
 and its marinade in batches and
 stir-fry for 3–4 minutes until cooked,
 adding more oil if needed.
4 Serve the chicken on a bed of
 Thai fragrant rice, with the peanut
 sauce poured over. Garnish with
 cilantro sprigs.

TRY THIS

For an easy alternative, replace
the chicken with pork cutlets or
flank steak, cut into thin strips.

Sesame Lamb

Prep time: 15 minutes
Cooking time: 15 minutes

2 cups fine fresh white bread crumbs
scant ½ cup sesame seeds
salt and freshly ground black pepper
1lb. (450g) lean boneless lamb, cut into
   ¼in. (0.5cm) thick slices
2 eggs, beaten
6 tbsp. peanut or sunflower oil
1 onion, sliced
3 carrots, cut into strips
2½ cups broccoli cut into florets
1in. (2.5cm) piece of fresh ginger,
   peeled and grated
2 cups (450ml) chicken stock
2 tbsp. dry sherry
1½ tbsp. cornstarch
1 tbsp. dark soy sauce
a few drops of sesame oil to serve

1 Mix the bread crumbs with the
  sesame seeds and season with
  salt and ground black pepper. Dip
  the lamb slices in the beaten egg,
  then coat them in the bread-crumb
  mixture, pressing the bread crumbs
  on firmly with your fingertips.

2 Heat 2 tbsp. oil in a wok or large
  skillet. Add half the lamb slices and
  fry for about 2 minutes on each side
  until golden. Remove from the pan,
  drain and keep warm. Cook the
  remaining lamb in the same way,
  using another 2 tbsp. oil.

3 Wipe the wok clean and heat the
  remaining oil. Add the onion,
  carrots, broccoli, and ginger and
  stir-fry for 2 minutes. Add the stock
  and sherry, cover, and cook the
  vegetables for 1 minute.

4 Blend the cornstarch and soy sauce
  with 1 tbsp. water. Stir the mixture
  into the wok and cook for 2 minutes,
  stirring constantly. Put the lamb
  slices back into the pan and cook for
  1–2 minutes until heated through.
  Sprinkle with sesame oil and serve.

TRY THIS

For an easy alternative, try this with
slices of turkey breast.

Serves 4

30 cal ♥ 1g protein
1.5g fat (trace sat)
2g fiber ♥ 3g carb ♥ 0g salt

10

75 cal ♥ 2g protein
6g fat (1g sat) ♥ 1g fiber
2g carb ♥ 0.1g salt

12

110 cal ♥ 2g protein
3g fat (trace sat) ♥ 0.8g fiber
19g carb ♥ 0.8g salt

14

224 cal ♥ 2g protein
13g fat (2g sat) ♥ 2g fiber
23g carb ♥ 0.7g salt

20

338 cal ♥ 37g protein
10g fat (3g sat) ♥ 2g fiber
27g carb ♥ 1.7g salt

34

215 cal ♥ 15g protein
13g fat (3g sat) ♥ 1g fiber
11g carb ♥ 1.2g salt

36

515 cal ♥ 40g protein
35g fat (25g sat) ♥ 1g fiber
9g carb ♥ 0.8g salt

40

318 cal ♥ 20g protein
20g fat (12g sat) ♥ 3g fiber
14g carb ♥ 0.3g salt

52

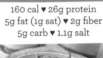

160 cal ♥ 26g protein
5g fat (1g sat) ♥ 2g fiber
5g carb ♥ 1.1g salt

54

397 cal ♥ 25g protein
25g fat (8g sat) ♥ 2g fiber
17g carb ♥ 0.4g salt

56

412 cal ♥ 21g protein
18g fat (3g sat) ♥ 2g fiber
46g carb ♥ 1.9g salt

72

403 cal ♥ 25g protein
10g fat (2g sat) ♥ 4g fiber
62g carb ♥ 0.7g salt

74

431 cal ♥ 12g protein
15g fat (3g sat) ♥ 2g fiber
61g carb ♥ 2.1g salt

78

451 cal ♥ 27g protein
13g fat (3g sat) ♥ 2g fiber
56g carb ♥ 2.6g salt

80

Calorie Gallery

450 cal ♥ 7g protein
21g fat (3g sat) ♥ 5g fiber
55g carb ♥ 2.1g salt

24

568 cal ♥ 11g protein
29g fat (4g sat) ♥ 6g fiber
65g carb ♥ 2.9g salt

26

334 cal ♥ 28g protein
11g fat ♥ 1g fiber
32g carb ♥ 4.0g salt

28

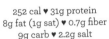

266 cal ♥ 12g protein
11g fat (2g sat) ♥ 0.6g fiber
33g carb ♥ 0.8g salt

30

252 cal ♥ 31g protein
8g fat (1g sat) ♥ 0.7g fiber
9g carb ♥ 2.2g salt

42

118 cal ♥ 28g protein
3g fat (0.5g sat) ♥ 4g fiber
13g carb ♥ 1.3g salt

44

247 cal ♥ 22g protein
16g fat (11g sat) ♥ 0.1g fiber
4g carb ♥ 0.8g salt

46

253 cal ♥ 31g protein
13g fat (9g sat) ♥ 0.4g fiber
2g carb ♥ 2.5g salt

48

660 cal ♥ 37g protein
31g fat (11g sat) ♥ 3g fiber
57g carb ♥ 1.6g salt

595 cal ♥ 30g protein
45g fat (24g sat) ♥ 2g fiber
18g carb ♥ 1.2g salt

58

60

339 cal ♥ 25g protein
11g fat (2g sat) ♥ 3g fiber
37g carb ♥ 0.4g salt

66

157 cal ♥ 4g protein
5g fat (1g sat) ♥ 1g fiber
22g carb ♥ 0.5g salt

70

476 cal ♥ 34g protein
8g fat (2g sat) ♥ 5g fiber
64g carb ♥ 3.4g salt

82

451 cal ♥ 35g protein
11g fat (2g sat) ♥ 4g fiber
59g carb ♥ 1.3g salt

84

335 cal ♥ 28g protein
4g fat (1g sat) ♥ 3g fiber
46g carb ♥ 1.0g salt

86

408 cal ♥ 18g protein
20g fat (5g sat) ♥ 2g fiber
38g carb ♥ 1.2g salt

88

306 cal ♥ 23g protein
11g fat (3g sat) ♥ 0.3g fiber
31g carb ♥ 2g salt

90

113 cal ♥ 3g protein
9g fat (1g sat) ♥ 3g fiber
6g carb ♥ 0.1g salt

94

167 cal ♥ 9g protein
11g fat (2g sat) ♥ 4g fiber
5g carb ♥ 1.6g salt

98

157cal ♥ 8g protein
9g fat (1g sat) ♥ 3g fiber
11g carb ♥ 1.1g salt

100

Calorie Gallery

334 cal ♥ 13g protein
11g fat (2g sat) ♥ 3g fiber
49g carb ♥ 1.5g salt

112

317 cal ♥ 2g protein
14g fat (2g sat) ♥ 0.6g fiber
43g carb ♥ 1.7g salt

114

334 cal ♥ 18g protein
8g fat (2g sat) ♥ 2g fiber
51g carb ♥ 3.5g salt

118

170 cal ♥ 21g protein
7g fat (1g sat) ♥ 3g fiber
11g carb ♥ 1.6g salt

134

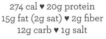

274 cal ♥ 20g protein
15g fat (2g sat) ♥ 2g fiber
12g carb ♥ 1g salt

138

279 cal ♥ 29g protein
15g fat (3g sat) ♥ 3g fiber
7g carb ♥ 0.4g salt

140

220 cal ♥ 23g protein
10g fat (3g sat) ♥ 2g fiber
8g carb ♥ 0.7g salt

672 cal ♥ 43g protein
18g fat (4.2g sat) ♥ 6g fiber
97g carb ♥ 0.7g salt

156

158

298 cal ♥ 26g protein
14g fat (4g sat) ♥ 3g fiber
15g carb ♥ 0.6g salt

160

275 cal ♥ 24g protein
16g fat (5g sat) ♥ 2g fiber
6g carb ♥ 2g salt

162

445 cal ♥ 11g protein
17g fat (9g sat) ♥ 3g fiber
60g carb ♥ 2g salt

02

136 cal ♥ 2g protein
7g fat (1g sat) ♥ 3g fiber
17g carb ♥ 2.5g salt

104

149 cal ♥ 4g protein
9g fat (1g sat) ♥ 3g fiber
14g carb ♥ 0.7g salt

108

232 cal ♥ 14g protein
18g fat (4g sat) ♥ 3g fiber
6g carb ♥ 0.9g salt

110

197 cal ♥ 30g protein
7g fat (1g sat) ♥ 1g fiber
6g carb ♥ 2g salt

22

335 cal ♥ 19g protein
25g fat (17g sat) ♥ 0.2g fiber
8g carb ♥ 1.6g salt

126

580 cal ♥ 24g protein
47g fat (24g sat) ♥ 2g fiber
27g carb ♥ 2.5g salt

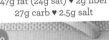

130

193 cal ♥ 22g protein
8g fat (1g sat) ♥ 2g fiber
7g carb ♥ 1.4g salt

132

312 cal ♥ 31g protein
19g fat (3g sat) ♥ 0.7g fiber
2g carb ♥ 1.5g salt

44

302 cal ♥ 21g protein
9g fat (3g sat) ♥ 4g fiber
36g carb ♥ 0.4g salt

672 cal ♥ 40g protein
30g fat (4g sat) ♥ 4g fiber
66g carb ♥ 2.9g salt

146

152

281 cal ♥ 21g protein
15g fat (3g sat) ♥ 3g fiber
16g carb ♥ 1.9g salt

154

210 cal ♥ 30g protein
8g fat (2g sat) ♥ 2g fiber
5g carb ♥ 0.9g salt

64

510 cal ♥ 41g protein
34g fat (12g sat) ♥ 0.5g fiber
9g carb ♥ 0.5g salt

166

661 cal ♥ 35g protein
41g fat (10g sat) ♥ 5g fiber
40g carb ♥ 2.3g salt

168

Index

PICTURE CREDITS
Photographers:
Steve Baxter (page 155);
Martin Brigdale (pages 11, 13, 1, 25,
41, 43, 49, 53, 55, 57, 59, 61, 67, 68,
69, 71, 73, 75, 79, 81, 83, 85, 87, 89,
91, 95, 99, 101, 103, 105, 109, 111, 113,
115, 119, 123, 127, 131, 135, 139, 141,
145, 147, 157, 161, 163, 167 and 169);
Nicki Dowey (pages 27, 31 and 47);
Gareth Morgans (pages 15, 35,
119, 159 and 165); Craig Robertson
(pages 9, 18T, 22, 37, 38, 64, 75, 106,
107, 120, 121, 124, 125, 128,
129, 136, 137, 142, 150 and 151);
Lucinda Symons (pages 16, 18B
and 153); Jon Whitaker (pages 29
and 45).

Home Economists:
Anna Bujrges-Lumsden,
Joanna Farrow, Emma Jane Frost,
Teresa Goldfinch, Alice Hart,
Lucy McKelvie, Kim Morphew,
Aya Nishimura, Katie Rogers,
Bridget Sargeson, Stella Sargeson,
Jennifer White and Mari Mererid
Wiliams.

Stylists:
Tamzin Ferdinando, Wei Tang,
Helen Trent and Fanny Ward.

CHEAP EATS
Budget-Busting Ideas That Won't Break the Bank

FLASH *in the* PAN
Spice Up Your Noodles & Stir-Fries

LET'S *do* BRUNCH
Mouth-Watering Meals to Start Your Day

PARTY FOOD
Delicious Recipes to Get the Party Started